Lectionary-Based
Gospel Dramas
for Lent
and the Easter Triduum

Lectionary-Based Gospel Dramas for Lent and the Easter Triduum

Sheila O'Connell-Roussell and
Therese Vorndran Nichols
Icons by Vicki Shuck

Saint Mary's Press
Christian Brothers Publications
Winona, Minnesota

Genuine recycled paper with 10% post-consumer waste.
Printed with soy-based ink.

The publishing team included Brian Singer-Towns, development editor; Cheryl Drivdahl, copy editor; Barbara Bartelson, production editor and typesetter; Cindi Ramm, design coordinator; Laurie Geisler, cover designer; Vicki Shuck, illustrator; pre-press, printing, and binding by the graphics division of Saint Mary's Press.

The scriptural quotations in this book are from the New Revised Standard Version of the Bible. Copyright © 1989 by the Division of Christian Education of the National Council of the Churches of Christ in the United States of America. All rights reserved. The quotation on page 15 is from Genesis 1:11, on page 47 from Psalm 109:14, on page 59 from John 12:28, on page 64 from Matthew 21:5, and on page 78 from Psalm 41:9–13.

All other scriptural material is freely paraphrased and is not to be used or understood as an official translation of the Bible. The first passage on page 107 is paraphrased from Isaiah 53:3–6, the second passage on page 107 from Isaiah 53:7, and the passage on page 121 from John 12:24–25.

Pope John Paul II's reflections about theater on page 8 are gleaned from *Collected Plays and Writings on Theater,* translated by Boleslaw Taborski (Berkeley: University of California Press, 1987).

The extract on pages 8–9 is quoted from *Decree on the Apostolate of Lay People (Apostolicum Actuositatem,* 1965), in *The Documents of Vatican II,* edited by Walter M. Abbott, SJ (New York: Guild Press, 1966), number 12. Copyright © 1966 by American Press.

The drama for the Third Sunday of Lent is adapted from *Herstory: The Mother's Tale,* a musical play by Sheila O'Connell-Roussell and Terri Vorndran Nichols (Bend, OR: Roger Nichols Music, 1992). Used with permission of the authors.

The drama for Passion Sunday, or Palm Sunday, is adapted in part from *Herstory* and in part from *The Word Is Made Flesh: The Sacred Art of Theatre,* by Sheila O'Connell-Roussell (Bend, OR: Amnchara Cruces, 1999). Used with permission of the author.

The dramas for Holy Thursday, for Good Friday, and for Holy Saturday and Easter Sunday are adapted in part from *Herstory.*

The prayer on pages 79 and 121 is quoted from *The Sacramentary,* English translation prepared by the International Commission on English in the Liturgy (New York: Catholic Book Publishing Company, 1985), page 545. Illustrations and arrangement copyright © 1985–1974 by Catholic Book Publishing Company, New York.

Printed in the United States of America

Printing: 9 8 7 6 5 4 3 2 1

Year: 2007 06 05 04 03 02 01 00 99

ISBN 0-88489-627-7

Contents

✝ ✝ ✝ ✝ ✝ ✝

We dedicate this book to our daughters, Shana O'Connell-Christman, and Claire Therese, Caroline Mary, and Caitlin Elizabeth Nichols, who are the incentive, inspiration, and catalyst for all our work. It is our lifelong commitment to share with them our most precious treasure—the gift of faith in Jesus and his mother. We also want to instill in them our belief that they—like all the children of the earth—are cherished by God.

Authors' Acknowledgments
We would like to thank the parishioners and pastoral staff of Saint Francis of Assisi Catholic Parish in Bend, Oregon, for their faith and confidence in our work and for letting us try out this project in so many "corners" of the vineyard—youth ministry, Rite of Christian Initiation of Adults, Scripture study, Re-membering Church, faith-sharing groups, liturgy of the word, classrooms, and as a journal for personal study.

In particular we would like to thank the youth of our parish who have sacrificed themselves to be our "test case" every Tuesday afternoon for the last two years. Early versions of this work were improved and clarified by their challenging comments. And much of our content has been developed in consideration of their questions and touching spiritual insights.

Our most heartfelt thanks goes to youth minister Scott Slattum, for his constant encouragement in this project, for his willingness to try out our material with his many youth groups, and for his critique and blessing. We remain in his debt.

We would also like to thank Saint Mary's Press and Carl Koch, for challenging us to attempt this work. Finally we want to express deep gratitude to Brian Singer-Towns, for his continual support and assurance, and for his patience and critical editing that have made this book what it is.

Introduction

Our Goal

Faith development and the conversion process have at their source our human hunger to know God and to discover what it means to be fully human. Catholic Tradition celebrates our profound relationship with Christ, who is truly God and truly human. In *Lectionary-Based Gospel Dramas for Lent and the Easter Triduum* our goal as authors is to employ all our skills, talents, and passion to explore and communicate this mystery of the Incarnation to young people through the medium of drama.

The Meaning of Lent and of the Easter Triduum

Although local customs in the universal church differ from country to country, since the Council of Nicaea in 325 C.E., Catholic Christians have observed the season of Lent to prepare for the paschal mysteries of the Easter Triduum. This is the great season of conversion. Those of us raised in the faith look deeply into our soul and recommit ourselves to our baptismal vows and to Christ. Our catechumens (unbaptized persons who wish to join our family of faith) are in the final weeks of their journey toward the celebration of the sacraments of initiation: baptism, the Eucharist, and confirmation.

Through the readings of the season of Lent, we honor the forty days Jesus spent in the desert fasting, praying, giving alms, and offering acts of charity to God. We remember that our life—with its cares and joys—is temporary. Every one of us will one day die and stand before our God. Our actions go before us. Our Lord stands beside us. In Lent, we attempt to become more conscious, to mark and honor the cycles of our lives and to remember that in all we say and do, Christ is in our midst.

The Power of Drama

One of the most powerful tools we have found for teaching, evangelizing, healing emotional wounds, inspiring changes of heart, and developing or enriching faith is the art of drama. We have experienced this firsthand through the strong, positive reactions to our two musical plays: *Herstory: The Mother's Tale,* which tells the story of Jesus through the memories of his mother and the other disciples, and *Back to Eden,* which spotlights the first man and woman, the glories of Creation, and God's unending love for us. As writers, we have been awed by the ability of drama to bring these stories to life.

His holiness Pope John Paul II spent many years as a playwright, theater critic, and actor. In his various writings on the theater, he professes the highest regard for drama's potential as a force for good. He observes that theater gives us insights that we cannot grasp in everyday life. Theater, he reflects, appeals not only to the mind but also to the senses and the heart, helping us to understand what it means to be fully human (Boleslaw Taborski, translator, *Collected Plays and Writings on Theater*).

Each drama in this book is meant to "break open" a Gospel passage and bring it to life, especially when the reading is dramatized shortly before it will be read from the pulpit at Mass. For example, in "Out of the Darkness, into the Light," the grieving sisters of Lazarus bemoan Jesus' failure to reach Bethany in time to bless their brother before he died. They wonder where Jesus was when they needed him. After Jesus finally arrives, he cries at the tomb with them, then calls back to life the dead friend whom he loves. The vivid unfolding of this drama may shed new insights on both the humanity and the divinity of Jesus presented in the liturgy of the word for the Fifth Sunday of Lent.

In "Lamb of God, Bread of Life," Jesus spends a beautiful evening with his closest friends. They gather together for Passover, the festival of freedom, a commemoration of the Exodus event in which God's people were saved. This night, the night before his death, Jesus promises that the freedom and redemption of Passover will soon be fulfilled in a way that surpasses their dreams. As he breaks the unleavened bread, he promises that he will be with them, and us, all throughout time, in the breaking of the bread. The Holy Thursday liturgy—and the precious gift of holy communion—may become more meaningful, more personal because of the dialog and action in this scene.

In like fashion, the rest of the dramas from this book can make the Gospel teachings "take flesh" and pass into people's hearts.

Special Features

Learning Style

Youth are the future of the church. They will hand on the flame of faith to succeeding generations. The teen and young adult years extend a magnificent challenge to those of us who are called to minister to youth as pastors, youth ministers, spiritual guides, mentors, teachers, parents, and guardians. In the prophetic text we know as the conciliar documents of Vatican II, the *Decree on the Apostolate of Lay People* calls us not only to minister to young people but also to enable them to minister to one another:

> Young persons exert very substantial influence on modern society. There has been a complete change in the circumstances of their lives, their mental attitudes, and their relationships with their own families. . . .

. . . As they become more conscious of their own personality, they are impelled by a zest for life and abounding energies to assume their own responsibility, and they yearn to *play their part* in social and cultural life. . . . *They themselves ought to become the prime and direct apostles of youth,* exercising the apostolate among themselves and through themselves and reckoning with the social environment in which they live. (No. 12; italics added)

Lectionary-Based Gospel Dramas uses the medium of drama to empower young people and adults to embrace their baptismal privilege to be catechists for one another and for themselves. To accomplish this goal, the leader's role in the presentation of the drama is purposefully minimal. Rather than lecturing, the leader simply provides the environment for learning.

The participants in the dramas function as catechist, lector, Gospel players, improv artists, small-group leaders, and audience. In these roles, the participants come in contact with a variety of images, emotions, moral dilemmas, and social settings, through which they meet flesh-and-blood persons and communities—imagined and historical—that encountered Jesus and the early church. Our intent is not only to teach the message of Jesus but also to weave within the icons, catechist sections, and role-playing, a sense of how the early community evangelized, articulated the roots of our sacramental celebrations, and developed the Gospels.

In combining use of the fine arts, the theater arts, and the arts of oral interpretation, speech, and improvisation with elements of cooperative learning, the participants share faith and teach one another about the liturgy and the Scriptures.

Leader's Tasks

General directions for the leader's tasks are provided on a resource located at the end of this introduction. Directions and information that are unique to each drama are located within the respective dramas. Of special note is the preparation of a costume trunk that contains clothing and props. A list of items needed is included at the beginning of each drama.

Icons

The icon for each drama is included not only for aesthetic value but also as an essential component of the learning experience. Although it is beneficial simply to experience and appreciate good art, as a learning tool an icon allows participants who are primarily visual learners to receive the information through a creative visual image. We intentionally used icons because they serve as an entry point to the sacred rather than as mere decoration for the page. We hope also that the use of icon art will encourage any developing artists in your midst to embrace their own vocation of celebrating spirituality through the arts.

The icons were created with a scratchboard technique. To use this technique, the artist begins with a black board. And like spiritual self-direction, in which a person consciously removes the darkness of resistance to the light of God's love, the artist slowly scratches off layer after layer of the black surface until the sacred image emerges.

Directions for using the icons with the participants are given in the leader's tasks resource at the end of this introduction.

The artist's caption for each icon and the Scripture citation or citations on which the icon is based are located on the same page as the icon.

Scheduling the Dramas

If you are a youth group leader or a catechist in a parish religious education program, *Lectionary-Based Gospel Dramas* can serve as a complete set of lessons to carry you from the first Sunday of Lent through Easter Sunday. As you meet with your group each time, drama after drama will draw your participants into the Gospel reading that awaits them in the upcoming Lenten or Easter Triduum liturgy. Usually youth groups and parish classes take a holiday break, just as schools do. If you do not have enough sessions to cover all the dramas, one option is to select certain dramas and save others for the following Lent and Easter. Another option is to incorporate elements from the dramas into special liturgies for your youth group or parishioners. You might even make certain dramas available for personal reflection at home, as an extension of your work together as a group.

If you are a schoolteacher, using the dramas once a week—especially on Fridays, when people are often tired—offers the students a solid yet fun entry into the world of the sacred Scriptures celebrated in the liturgies of the seasons. However, Easter vacations may break into that neat format. Use your judgment about the best timing for incorporating the dramas when this occurs. We also suggest that you adapt the dramas for use in any special liturgies and prayer services that you coordinate for the season.

The three dramas for the Easter Triduum present a problem for weekly parish programs and even for schools, because they relate to liturgies that occur within the same week. You may wish to spread these dramas out by using the Good Friday drama earlier during Lent, replacing one of the Lenten Sunday dramas. The Holy Thursday drama could be used the week before Holy Week or during Holy Week itself. The Holy Saturday and Easter Sunday drama could be used after Holy Week, when students return from Easter break, as a reflection on the great mystery of Christ's Resurrection.

Our Gift and Our Hope

The icons and dramas in this book are the fruit of our study, meditation, and prayer. Using the personal reflections of our life journeys, as well as our experience in the classroom and parish ministry, we believe we have developed a teaching tool that will sustain, strengthen, and support you in your critical vocation of proclaiming the Gospel. Our belief is that the Gospel of Jesus has the power to transform lives. Our hope and prayer is that you find *Lectionary-Based Gospel Dramas* to be the gift that it has been to our teaching mission.

Leader's Tasks

Preparation for the Drama

1. Photocopy the script and distribute a copy to each participant.
2. Begin the session by inviting the participants to take a few minutes of silence to view and reflect on the icon.
3. Briefly explain the nature of icons and then lead a reflection and discussion using the following, or similar, words:

   > An icon is an image that invites us to see and enter into the realm of the Spirit. This icon is the artist's expression of the readings we celebrate today. As you gaze at the icon, what feelings, thoughts, ideas, or issues come to mind? How does the art make you feel? Would anyone like to share any of the thoughts or feelings that the icon inspires in them?

   > As part of the reflection and discussion, or as closure to the discussion, you might want to read the artist's icon caption from the bottom of the page.

4. After the group discussion subsides, ask participants to volunteer for the roles in the Gospel drama. The roles are listed with each drama. If your group is small, ask some volunteers to assume more than one role.
5. Direct the volunteers to search through the costume trunk for articles of clothing and props that will embellish their portrayal of the drama.

Presentation of the Drama

Explain to the participants that throughout the drama, the catechist will stand before the group as narrator of the scene and minister of hospitality, who welcomes the audience, introduces the lector, and cues the players and the audience.

Follow-up After the Drama

1. At the conclusion of the drama, ask the audience for a round of applause for the catechist, the lector, and the Gospel players.
2. Thank everyone, and invite the catechist to lead a discussion of the reflection questions. Assist the catechist by facilitating the group discussion when necessary and by adding your own comments. Reflection questions are provided for each drama.

Improv

If time permits, direct the Gospel players to take ten minutes or so by themselves to prepare an improv that portrays, in a contemporary fashion, the teachings and main points of the day's discussion. When the Gospel players are ready, have them perform the improvised skit.

Closure

1. Invite the participants' questions or comments prompted by the icon, the drama, the discussion, and the improvised skit.
2. Offer any closing comments or announcements. If the drama has taken place before the liturgy in which the dramatized Gospel passages will be read, remind the participants to be attentive to the readings during the celebration. If you are planning another Gospel drama for the next session, give the participants the Scripture readings for that drama so that they can read the passages in preparation for the next session.
3. Close the session by inviting the participants to offer a traditional or spontaneous closing prayer.

Illustration by Vicki Shuck

First Sunday of Lent Icon

Filled with the Spirit and focused on his commitment to God, Jesus recognizes the voice of the Tempter. Even when we are weak, the Spirit helps us to hear the voice of God and gives us strength to stand up to temptations.
A: Matthew 4:1–11; B: Mark 1:12–15; C: Luke 4:1–13

First Sunday of Lent

Gospel Readings and Themes

Cycle A. Matthew 4:1–11. Tempted in the desert: preparation for the mission.

Cycle B. Mark 1:12–15. Put to the test: temptation in the desert.

Cycle C. Luke 4:1–13. Led by the Spirit: forty days and forty nights.

Preparation for the Drama

(See resource intro–A, "Leader's Tasks.")

Roles

Catechist, who coordinates the drama

Lector, who leads the opening prayer and proclaims the sacred Scriptures

Gospel players, who enflesh the roles in the scriptural drama

- Jesus
- John the Baptist (nonspeaking role)
- Voice from Heaven
- Evil One (the Tempter)

Costume Trunk Items

A lectionary or Bible, robes, headdresses, a liquor bottle, and food items

Presentation of the Drama
(See resource intro–A, "Leader's Tasks.")

Script for the Background Reading

Catechist. During the season of Lent, we are called to re-examine our goals and values; to recommit to our baptismal vows; to turn away from evil; and to embrace the Light, who is Christ, and enter the Reign of God. The Gospel this Sunday tells the story of Jesus' forty days and forty nights in the desolation of the Judean wasteland, where he defeats the temptation of the Evil One. This sojourn is placed at the very beginning of the public ministry of Jesus in the Gospel and at the beginning of our liturgical readings for Lent. In the desert Christ forms and clarifies a plan to reconcile humanity with his Father. Within the story is an invitation to each of us to examine the deserts of our life. Great wisdom is woven into this memory of Jesus passed down through the ages. It is a pathway to freedom. The story of Jesus' temptation in the desert is a blueprint for resisting evil by holding fast to the truth. And Jesus has promised that the truth will set us free.

Script for the Gospel Reading

[The lector leads everyone in prayer while holding up a lectionary or Bible for all to see.]

Lector. Come, Holy Spirit. Teach us wisdom so that we may always have the ability to discern what is right and what is wrong. Enlighten our hearts and minds and give us a hunger for your will for our lives.

[The lector proclaims the Gospel reading for the current cycle from the lectionary or Bible. Upon finishing, the lector leads the group in response to the Gospel, again holding up the lectionary or Bible for all to see.]

Lector. The Gospel of our Lord Jesus Christ.

Group. Thanks be to God.

Script for the Gospel Drama

[The catechist announces to the group the title of the Gospel scene to be dramatized.]

Catechist. "Who Are You, Anyway?"

[The catechist describes the Gospel scene to the group.]

Catechist. As we begin this drama, let's imagine Jesus telling his disciples what happened the day the Evil One approached him. Only two people could tell that story, Jesus and the Tempter. This is Jesus' version. The Apostles passed it from one community to another, and over time their memories formed the sacred writings we know as the Gospels. We, disciples of Christ at the genesis of the third millennium, share it with you. You will tell your children. And so the cycle of redemption passes from generation to generation. The Gospel is proclaimed to the ends of the earth.

[Jesus and John the Baptist walk silently into the scene.]

The story begins with Jesus approaching his cousin John for the baptism of repentance in the Jordan River. Immediately the Holy Spirit descends on the Christ and a voice from heaven proclaims:

Voice from Heaven. This is my beloved Son, in whom I am well pleased.

Catechist. Filled with the Spirit, Jesus travels into the Jordanian desert, to be alone with God, to prepare himself for his mission as the Messiah.

In the dusty desert wasteland where the sun blisters the bare rocks, Jesus faces the test of temptation. In the Garden of Eden, God had said:

Voice from Heaven. "Let the earth put forth vegetation: plants yielding seed, and fruit trees of every kind on earth that bear fruit." . . . Yes, it is good.

Catechist. The dry barrenness of the Jordanian wilderness seems to stand in direct contrast with the beauty of the Garden of Eden. But to the Jews, the desert is an ancient image of both danger and hope. It is in the desert wasteland of our lives that God "hears our cry," offers salvation, and leads us into the land of promise. It was in the desert that Israel was called out of the slavery of Egypt into freedom, given the Covenant of the Law, and healed of idolatry.

Jesus is praying quietly to himself when the Evil One approaches. The Evil One, the Tempter, sits down beside Jesus and begins a conversation.

Evil One (the Tempter). Hey! How you doing? Hot out here, isn't it. Oh, I would say about 110 in the shade. *[Brandishing a liquor bottle]* Want some tequila? a little lime juice and firewater over ice? Hmm?

Jesus. No, thank you.

Evil One. Hey! How'd you like a taco?

Jesus. No, thank you.

Evil One. *[Holding out a variety of food items]* Some matzo, maybe? lox, bagels . . . a little cream cheese?

Jesus. No, thank you.

Evil One. What? Are you weird?! You don't eat?! You don't drink?! What? My food . . . my booze . . . aren't good enough for you? Listen! I happen to know that you're starving. As a matter of fact, you could eat a horse right now, couldn't you? Forty days, forty nights. What?! Are you playing Noah out here in this God-forsaken hellhole of a desert?

Catechist. In the Gospel reading for today, God uses the desert experience as an allegory, or symbol, to talk to us about how life and Mother Earth have changed since the Creator made us.

Voice from Heaven. When I created the heavens and the earth, the earth was a green, lush, beautiful place, where man and woman ate freely from the tree of life. Now look, children; the Evil One has deforested and destroyed my garden, turned it into yellowed, desolate, crumbling limestone, a blistering wilderness. And you have used your free will to let that happen. So I have sent my Son to lead you home to my love, to heal everything and make it new. The day of the Lord is at hand.

Catechist. Jesus, the Tree of Life, stands in the arid desert. He is Living Water for the thirsty. He is Christ, the Bread of Life, offering the Eucharist to the hungry. Truth, courage, and loyalty to God's will for freedom clash against the temptations of the Evil One, eternally offering only compromise and bondage.

As our scene continues, Jesus is in prayer. The Evil One tries to distract him. Jesus resists his tricks by focusing on his own relationship with his Father, God. Putting our mind and heart on the love of God is always the way to resist temptation.

Evil One. Look, let me be straight with you. You seem like the kind of man who appreciates honesty. I just wanna know who I'm dealing with. So here goes. There's talk around here that you're him. Are you? Are you the Promised One? The Son of God? If you're the Anointed One, . . . command these little round pieces of limestone to become loaves of bread. I'm running out of bagels for this lox. . . . Great lox; . . . I could use a little bread. Are you the kind of guy who'd feed the hungry? You know, food is a little scarce this time of year.

Jesus. Father, when my ancestors were hungry, you sent them bread from heaven. When they were thirsty, water rushed from the rocks, and you gave them possession of a Land of Promise. Blessed be the name of the Lord.

[The Evil One gestures to the catechist his disgust with this man in the desert and then focuses back on Jesus.]

Evil One. All this poetry is nice, Holy One, but you've gotta be hungry. Spiritual food is deep, really deep, but you could probably use a little bite of something to chew on, eh? Whatta ya say? I know I'm starving! Help me! How about turning this stone into a little piece of bread. Hmm? Staff of life. Can't live without it.

Jesus. It's written that a person doesn't live by bread alone.

Evil One. Good. You know the Scriptures. Book of Deuteronomy, right? Well, isn't it the truth. Said a long time ago, in another desert, by another prophet. Moses, right? The Boss Man humbled all of you by letting you hunger in the Sinai. Yeah! Yeah! I've heard all about it.

Jesus. Blessed be the name of the Lord.

Evil One. Ah! The Great I Am caused manna to fall from the sky. For forty years, there it was. Manna for breakfast. Bread of life at first light. So, what do you think? Did it do any good? Forget basic bread. How about a sub, hunk of hoagie, little cracker and cheese?

Jesus. One does not live by bread alone, but by the Word of God.

Evil One. Remember the visions of Isaiah? Bread raining down from heaven for you? It's gonna be some kind of golden age when the Messiah comes. You could have a little bread. Multiply a few loaves if you wanted. Rain down bread. People will follow you. You'll be so popular . . .

Jesus. For those in bondage, I pray. Come out from the darkness. You shall not hunger or thirst, neither scorching wind nor sun shall strike you, for God—who has pity—will lead you to rushing springs of living water. Children of my Father, drink fully of the river of life. The path of satisfaction is dependence on God, not anything of this earth.

Evil One. You're an interesting kind of guy. I really like your seamless cloak. A robe like that is pretty rare—and expensive. Whoever gave it to you must really like you. You're that Jesus, aren't you? I've heard a lot about you. You're a pretty impressive dude. Not very talkative though.

Jesus. Wisdom teaches that in the presence of strangers, you should do nothing that is to be kept secret, for you never know what they will divulge. Wisdom suggests that you not reveal your thoughts to anyone, in order to protect happiness. It's not wise to cast your pearls before swine.

Evil One. Okay! So you like being mysterious—I can handle that! I like a good mystery, a good challenge. *[Pause]* You know, we haven't actually met, but I've been following your career all along. I like keeping records on people like you. There's been a lot of talk about you since the day you were born—actually since you were conceived. Son of the carpenter . . . Son of Virgin Mary . . . Son of God? Do you know who I am, Jesus? I'm the one who can make something out of you. If you follow me, you won't be riding on the back of a jackass. You won't be hanging out with a bunch of worthless fishermen. You'll own a fleet of chariots and dine with Caesar himself. And let us not forget the wealth, the power and pleasures that come with privilege.

Jesus. There is a proverb that teaches that wisdom is better than jewels. Prudence, knowledge, and discretion are true wealth. The Law of Moses says to remember the Lord your God, for it is God who gives you real power.

Evil One. Maybe so. But my world can be very entertaining, very pleasurable for a long, long time. The future is yours for the taking. *[The Evil One gestures to Jesus to look into the future.]* All the kingdoms of the world and more I will give to you, if you worship me.

Jesus. The word of God commands that you shall worship the Lord your God, and only God shall you serve.

Evil One. Why, you self-righteous Galilean! Just who do you think you are? Who do you think you're talking to? You know, you're a lot like your mother. Yeah! You sound just like her.

[The Evil One mysteriously waves his hands. Jesus and he instantly find themselves looking down into the city of Jerusalem from the highest roof of the Temple.]

Do you know where you are, Carpenter? In one heartbeat I transported you to the highest rooftop of the Temple of Jerusalem. Not bad, eh! From the deepest desert to the center of the city in a second . . .

Catechist. The Evil One challenges Jesus to a battle of wits designed to tempt him to commit the sin of pride. The devil tries to get Jesus to proclaim his own power. But Jesus dispels the seduction of evil by relying on the power of God.

Evil One. Look, you can see the golden hills of Hebron from up here. And look! You can see the courtyard of the Temple. Go on, Promised One, look down.

I know! Why don't you do one of your God tricks? I did a trick for you. . . . Show me your stuff. Go on, Son of God. Throw yourself down, and let's see what happens. You know where you are, don't you?

Jesus. Have mercy, O Lord, on Jerusalem, the city of your sanctuary. Zion has seen your majesty, and your Temple, your glory. The time is at hand. Father, fulfill the prophecies spoken in your name. Wisdom has built her house. . . . Like the morning star among the clouds, like the full moon at the festal season; like the sun shining on the Temple of the Most High, the majesty of your Temple, O Lord, gives praise to your name.

Evil One. What are you, a poet? Don't get carried away on me now. Get real! This place is great. Look around, Christ. Think of the power wielded in this place. We're standing on the parapet of the Temple of David, built by Solomon, rebuilt after the Captivity in Babylon and restored by Herod the Great. Have you met his son Antipas? Hmm? You will.

Jesus. And the Lord said: "My shepherd shall do my will. The foundations of my Temple will be laid. Jerusalem will be rebuilt." Father, I come to do your will.

Evil One. Why shouldn't you stand here? This is the place where every morning a priest blows the trumpet that proclaims the first light of the dawn, to announce the hour of sacrifice. So why shouldn't you leap! Right into the Temple court. Aren't you the *Perfect Sacrifice of your Abba Daddy?* Go on, amaze everybody. Didn't prophet Malachi say that you would suddenly come to the Temple? Well a flying entrance from the parapet would be sudden. It would prove that you're the One, the Chosen Son. They'd all believe in you then. Why shouldn't you do it? A little publicity never hurt anybody. Are you afraid, Son of God?

Jesus. Fear of the Lord is the beginning of wisdom. . . . Humility goes before honor. Blessed are you, Father, in the Temple of your holy glory. Blessed is your throne, where cherubim praise and exalt your name. Father, be glorified in your Son.

Evil One. It's getting really *thick* around here! Speaking of my pals, the cherubim: This book you keep quoting also says that your famous Father will send his angels to protect you. On their hands they will hold you up, so you won't hurt your tender feet on these stones. Now that would be very impressive. I would really like to see that. I used to hang out with those guys. Come on! Give it a try and call on your angel friends. This will be great. A hit! A MAJOR HIT!

Jesus. You shall not tempt the Lord, your God.

Catechist. Many times the English language keeps us from grasping the rich meaning behind a passage in the Scriptures. The word *temptation* is a good example. In modern English, it means "the act of seducing, persuading, enticing, or luring into evil." The Greek word from which it was translated in the Bible is *peirazein,* which includes the idea of testing for preparation. The purpose of this testing is to build strength, not to trick or lead into sin. The test is in front of us at all times. The question is, Will we walk through the fire and become strong, tempered like the purest gold, or will we weaken and be destroyed?

Jesus. Begone, Satan!

Evil One. Okay, if you say so. . . . But I'll be back.

Catechist. The struggle against evil is a continual challenge we face every day of our lives. But the victory of Jesus is our birthright as children of God, as followers of Christ. The life, death, and Resurrection of Jesus have long been studied by his followers as a blueprint for understanding the challenges of the Christian life. The Gospel celebrated on the first Sunday of Lent is a window through which we can see the personal trials and temptations that faced Jesus.

Jesus teaches us to use the gift of our free will, given to us as creatures made in the image of God, to refuse to enter into a battle of wills with evil. Jesus shows us that relying on the truth of the revealed Word of God in the Scriptures and sacraments is our defense in the battle for justice.

When Jesus told the devil to begone, the Evil One gave up and left him. Jesus then returned to his home in Nazareth and entered the synagogue to pray for his mission. It has been twenty-five hundred years since the community of Isaiah wrote the inspired words of his prayer, and two thousand years since Jesus took the book of the prophet and read them there in the synagogue. The words still stir great power, love, and hope for humanity.

Jesus. The Spirit of the Lord is upon me, because God has anointed me to preach the Good News to the poor. God has sent me to proclaim release to the captives and recovering of sight to the blind, to liberate the oppressed, to proclaim a year of Jubilee.

Today this scripture is fulfilled in your hearing.

Follow-up After the Drama

(See resource intro–A, "Leader's Tasks.")

Reflection Questions

- Has anyone ever tempted you to participate in something that you knew was wrong? If so, how did you handle the situation?
- How does evil try to seduce us to do wrong?
- How did Jesus overcome the temptation to sin? What can we learn from that?
- What does this Gospel tell us about who Jesus is? about his character and nature?

Improv
(See resource intro–A, "Leader's Tasks.")

Closure
(See resource intro–A, "Leader's Tasks.")

Second Sunday of Lent Icon

Heaven meets earth as the Apostles awaken to see a transfigured Jesus standing with Moses and Elijah and hear the voice of God proclaiming Jesus as the Beloved Son. We pray that our inner eyes may be open to know the glory of God that is always present to us. A: Matthew 17:1–9; B: Mark 9:2–10; C: Luke 9:28–36

Second Sunday of Lent

Gospel Readings and Themes

Cycle A. Matthew 17:1–9. Transformed before their eyes.
Cycle B. Mark 9:2–10. The Transfiguration: Jesus, the Son of man.
Cycle C. Luke 9:28–36. Moses and Elijah proclaim the glory of God.

Preparation for the Drama
(See resource intro–A, "Leader's Tasks.")

Roles

Catechist, who coordinates the drama
Lector, who leads the opening prayer and proclaims the sacred Scriptures
Gospel players, who enflesh the roles in the scriptural drama
- James
- Jesus
- John
- Peter
- Moses
- Elijah
- Voice from Heaven

Costume Trunk Items

A lectionary or Bible, four ordinary robes (for James, John, Peter, and Jesus), three white robes (for Jesus, to be worn under his ordinary robe, and for Moses and Elijah), headdresses, and a scroll representing the Torah

Presentation of the Drama
(See resource intro–A, "Leader's Tasks.")

Script for the Background Reading

Catechist. The synoptic Gospels of Matthew, Mark, and Luke tell the story of the Transfiguration of Jesus. This scene in the Gospel foreshadows one of Jesus in resurrected glory. Witnessed by Peter, James, and John, it proclaims Jesus in his divine nature. It connects him to the tradition of the covenant of Abraham, the salvation tradition of Moses, and the prophetic ministry of Elijah. And it identifies Jesus as the Son of God.

To the Jewish Apostles who witness this mystical encounter, the Transfiguration is a clear message from God that "the time is at hand," the Messiah is among them. The mission of Jesus and the mission of John the Baptist are proclaimed by two significant prophets, Moses and Elijah. The Apostles—like you and me at the beginning of our spiritual life—are asleep, so they are unaware of the reality of heaven all around them. Only after awakening and seeing the glory of the presence of the Lord do they begin to understand, in awe and amazement, what they are experiencing.

They are frightened when the cloud of God's presence covers them, proclaiming: "This is my Son, my Chosen. Listen to him!" Jesus, who is the Way, the Truth, and the Life, will lead us to his Father, if we are willing to follow. Like Peter, James, and John, if we awaken ourselves to recognize the reality of the Lord's presence among us, if we are willing to follow Jesus into the mystery of God in our lives, and if we listen to the teachings of Jesus, the Son of God, we will be transformed. The Reign of God is at hand.

Script for the Gospel Reading

[The lector leads everyone in prayer while holding up a lectionary or Bible for all to see.]

Lector. Lord Jesus, we ask to follow you into the cloud of unknowing, into the mystery of your glory. Make us a people who are willing to be transformed into who we were created to be—children of God. Open us to your presence and awaken us to your will for our lives.

[The lector proclaims the Gospel reading for the current cycle from the lectionary or Bible. Upon finishing, the lector leads the group in response to the Gospel, again holding up the lectionary or Bible for all to see.]

Lector. The Gospel of our Lord Jesus Christ.

Group. Thanks be to God.

Script for the Gospel Drama

[The catechist announces to the group the title of the Gospel scene to be dramatized.]

Catechist. "The Cloud of Unknowing"

[The catechist describes the Gospel scene to the group.]

Catechist. Our drama begins with the Apostles Peter, James, and John as they follow Jesus up a mountainside. Like those first disciples, we follow Jesus into the cloud of the unknown. They think they are taking a hike. But they are about to experience a profound mystical encounter between the Lord and the Father. They are about to witness the Transfiguration of Jesus, a vision of Jesus' true nature as the Anointed One, the incarnate Son of God, Second Person of the Blessed Trinity.

What the Apostles Peter, James, and John are going to experience will take them a lifetime to understand. It is only in reflecting back on our experiences with God that we can come to understand their meaning. In the present moment, God's hand in our lives can be confusing, *a cloud of unknowing.*

James. Fourteen miles from Caesarea Philippi, without a stop. It's quite a hike. What are we doing? The Lord's so quiet. Peter, he hasn't said a word for hours. We just keep walking and walking. Oh, my feet.

John. This isn't a walk, James. Mount Hermon is ninety-four hundred feet high; I don't call this a walk. We're climbing a mountain. Can't you feel your calves screaming?

James. You're such a child, John. Peter, why did you bring this boy with us?

Peter. The Lord wanted him. Stop complaining and look at the view. You can actually see the Dead Sea from up here. You can see all the way to the other end of Palestine. That's a hundred miles away. The Creator did such a good job. This is beautiful.

James. Lord, Lord! Look, we can see Qumran. Way over there. That's where those disgruntled Sadducees who say the Temple is corrupt have built their world out in the desert. I've always wanted to go there.

John. What makes you think that they'd let you in? *[He laughs.]*

James. Where are we going?

Peter. I don't know, but if we're following Jesus, we're going to the right place. *[They all laugh.]* Come on, follow him.

James. The weather's starting to change. It's like there's a storm moving in . . .

Peter. Definite turbulence. Is that lightning? Those clouds are moving in on the mountaintop.

John. I can hardly see you guys anymore, the fog's so thick.

James. John, you live in a cloud.

Catechist. The mysterious cloud of unknowing is an ancient sacred symbol to the Jewish people. The presence of God is remembered as manifesting from within a cloud. It's a way of saying, We see God's presence, but only surrounded with mystery.

In Jewish salvation history, God led the people in their Exodus wanderings in the desert with a pillar of cloud by day and a pillar of fire by night. When Moses received the tablets of the Law, the Ten Commandments, on Mount Sinai, God spoke from within a cloud. Later in their wanderings, when the Hebrews built a tent to honor the presence of God in the tabernacle, a cloud covered the tent and the glory of the Lord filled the tabernacle. When, finally, Solomon built and dedicated the Temple of David, a mysterious, luminous cloud filled the house of the Lord. All through the Old Testament, the image of the cloud is used to show the mysterious presence of Wisdom, the Shechinah, the Spirit, the glory of God.

John. I'm going to follow Jesus all my life. But does he have to lead us straight up a mountainside? I was looking forward to a little excitement in the city. I thought we were going to Jerusalem. My feet hurt.

James. If we're going to follow him, we go where he goes. Following Jesus isn't just a party.

John. We have gone to a lot of great parties with Jesus. Remember the one with the guy . . . What is his name? We went to his house. You remember?

Peter. I'm sure there'll be other parties. Jesus loves a good party. Today, we climb a mountain.

John. Why a mountain? Why can't he lead us to the beach?

James. The beach would be nice.

John. Why a mountain? Why this mountain? It's getting dark, and we're on a mountain.

Peter. Thank God, he's stopping.

James. I think he's resting.

Peter. You know the Lord. He's praying.

John. Well, I'm going to take a little nap. Wake me when he's done. *[Yawn]*

Peter. We could all use a little rest. *[Yawn]*

Catechist. Like the cloud of unknowing, the mountaintop has always been a sacred image to the Jewish people. When Moses met God and received the tablets of the Law, it was on the top of Mount Sinai. When Elijah sought God, he found him not in the wind, not in an earthquake, but in a whisper on the top of Mount Horeb. Meeting God is always a mountaintop experience.

Today, on the Mount of Transfiguration, Jesus is to more fully understand his mission. Moses and Elijah will confirm what he knows in his soul.

As Jesus prays on the mountaintop while Peter, James, and John sleep, he is joined by Moses, the greatest teacher and lawgiver, and Elijah, the greatest mystic, prophet, and miracle worker. Moses and Elijah approach Jesus as he searches for God in the cloud of unknowing. They know who Jesus is. During their lives on earth, they prayed for and foretold the time of Messiah's coming. And now, the Day of the Lord is at hand.

Jesus. *[Removing his ordinary outer robe to reveal the white robe beneath it]* Father God, I stand before you, your Son, willing to do your will. I have prepared myself in the desert, studied and prayed. I have gathered together my Apostles and disciples to join this mission to proclaim the Reign of God. It is time to accomplish your will in Jerusalem. I pray for guidance, discernment, and direction as I plan to take this step. I surround myself with your great saints and ask their help as I begin my public ministry.

Catechist. As Jesus prays, the cloud parts and Jesus sees Moses and Elijah.

[A bright light may be shone on Jesus while he speaks with Moses and Elijah.]

Moses. *[Carrying a scroll representing the Torah]* Son of the Great I Am . . . it is a privilege to speak with you.

Elijah. Living Water . . . we have waited for your coming. The time is at hand. The people of Jerusalem thirst for your wisdom.

Moses. Their souls hunger. You are the Bread from Heaven that will satisfy their hearts. You are the Manna offered by God in the desert of their bondage. Free them . . . lead them back to the love of your Father.

Elijah. Teach them the justice that God demands for the earth. The time is at hand. You are Emmanuel. The Day of the Lord has dawned. God has given me permission to bless the ministry of your cousin John the Baptizer. John is the voice crying out in the wilderness. Prepare the way for the coming of the Lord. John has proclaimed the coming of Messiah, the Son of Man. You are God's Anointed.

Moses. You are the Chosen One, the Breath of Hope for the earth . . . the Fire of Love that burns in our hearts. You are the Waters of Life. . . . Call the people out of bondage. Offer them freedom, salvation from the slavery of sin, for the Reign of God is at hand. Your departure, which you will accomplish at Jerusalem, will call them home.

Catechist. The Gospel stories were originally written in Greek. In that language, the departure of which Moses speaks can be translated as an exodus. Entering Jerusalem is an exodus for Jesus and for us. The people of God are being called out of bondage into a new freedom in Christ. We are called to live in the land of promise as God's family of the church. To follow Jesus, we have to leave all the situations and addictions that steal our freedom and keep us enslaved. We are invited to follow Jesus in complete trust on the journey into an adventure called new life.

Elijah. It is time to enter Jerusalem, the city of the prophets.

Moses. Jerusalem . . . the city of God's Temple.

Elijah. Beware the house of Jezebel.

Moses. Beware the plagues of bondage.

Catechist. Peter, James, and John awake from a heavy sleep to witness the presence of Moses and Elijah speaking with Jesus. And they are amazed by what they see.

John. Peter, James, wake up! Something's going on here. Peter, wake up!

Peter. What is happening?

James. Leave me alone, John. Peter, I told you to leave him home. John, what do you want?

John. Look at the Rabbi. He looks all weird.

Peter. Oh, my Lord! It's like the prophet Daniel described. His hair white as wool . . .

James. Jesus is all white, all lit up. His garments are dazzling white. Peter, what does this mean?

Peter. The prophet described the coming of the Son of man, the human person who would be the glory of God.

John. Those guys . . . who are those guys with him?! The one with the scroll . . . the other one?

Peter. Listen. Can you hear anything, James?

James. No. I'm terrified. I've never seen anything like this in all my life. I think the one without the scroll is Elijah. Oh, Lord. Does that mean the end of the world is at hand?! Elijah is supposed to return at the end of the world.

John. We will have to ask Jesus about Elijah—about the end of the world.

Peter. The prophet carrying the Torah is Moses . . . I'm sure of it.

John. This is amazing. We have been permitted to witness the meeting, the coming together, of the greatest saints of our tradition.

Peter. Who is this Jesus we follow? Even our great lawgiver Moses and the holy prophet Elijah pay him homage.

Jesus, Lord, thank you for the privilege of seeing this day. I know now that you have come to herald a new age, a time of gathering together your followers.

John. You asked us to be fishers—gatherers of humanity.

Peter. It is only fitting that we prepare the booths for the feast of tabernacles . . .

Catechist. For the Apostles this is a moment of fear of the Lord. Not the kind of fear that means being afraid of God, but fear in the sense that what is happening is beyond understanding. The Apostles stand in awe before profound glory.

In ancient times the Jews used a booth—that is, a tent—to create sacred space when they were away from Jerusalem. Peter wants to honor the Lord and the sacred experience they have just shared together; he wants to set up booths, or portable tabernacles.

Peter. One booth for you, Lord; one for Moses; and one for Elijah. We will pray and worship the God of the Covenant together in the sacred place in this holy of holies.

James. Jesus, you are the true tabernacle of God's presence. We wish to build a shrine to commemorate this day.

John. To remember forever how God covered us with the divine presence in this place.

Catechist. And as the Spirit of God covers them with a cloud of the divine presence, a voice proclaims from within the cloud so that all can hear:

Voice from Heaven. This is my Son, my Chosen. Listen to him!

John. My Chosen? The voice said, "My Son, my Chosen!"

James. A voice from heaven asks me to listen? With the psalmist, I pray, that I might be still, and know God.

Peter. Lord, you are the Son of God.

Catechist. When the voice has spoken, Moses and Elijah disappear and Jesus is once again alone with Peter, James, and John.

Peter. Lord, I don't want to leave here. I'm never going to be the same after witnessing such glory. How can I go about the ordinary everyday of life after seeing your glory?

James. Peter, we will never forget this moment together. We will never forget that our Lord is the Promised One. This will give us strength to do our work.

John. The Word of God is among us. We have heard the Word, seen the Light. Jesus is the Light of the World.

Peter. Jesus has permitted us to see this moment of glory for the sake of those who will join our mission later. No gift is given except for the building of the community. We can't talk about this except among ourselves. But one day we will proclaim it to the world, to the ends of the earth.

Catechist. And they keep silent and tell no one what they have seen, for it is most difficult to find words to describe an experience of the Spirit. The Gospel records the community's memory that Jesus ordered the Apostles to keep their experience of his Transfiguration to themselves until after the Resurrection. The Transfiguration can only be understood through the eyes of faith.

Follow-up After the Drama

(See resource intro–A, "Leader's Tasks.")

Reflection Questions

- How does the Transfiguration help us understand who Jesus is and what he came to teach?
- How does Jesus challenge us to transform, or change, our life?
- What would you have thought if you had been with Peter, James, and John that day?
- When Jesus shared with the Apostles his mystical encounter with Moses and Elijah, what was he trying to show them about their future mission?
- How can we become more awake in our vocation to follow Jesus?
- What is the purpose of prayer in our life?

Improv
(See resource intro–A, "Leader's Tasks.")

Closure
(See resource intro–A, "Leader's Tasks.")

Illustration by Vicki Shuck

Third Sunday of Lent Icon

God's mercy is revealed when Jesus shares the truth of himself with the scorned woman at the well, throws the money changers out of the holy Temple, and tells the parable of the fig tree. A: John 4:5–42; B: John 2:13–25; C: Luke 13:1–9. This drama focuses on the readings for cycles A and B.

Third Sunday of Lent

The readings for the three cycles of this Sunday are so rich that we could not combine them into a single drama. This drama reflects only the Gospel stories from cycles A and B of the lectionary. Note that if your parish has an RCIA program, this is a scrutiny Sunday. The scrutinies always use the cycle A readings.

Gospel Readings and Themes

Cycle A. John 4:5–42. The Samaritan woman at the well: Living Water.
Cycle B. John 2:13–25. My Father's house: warning the sellers in the Temple.

Preparation for the Drama
(See resource intro–A, "Leader's Tasks.")

Roles

Catechist, who coordinates the drama
Lector, who leads the opening prayer and proclaims the sacred Scriptures
Gospel players, who enflesh the roles in the scriptural drama
- Samaritan Woman
- Joab
- Ruth the Neighbor
- Jesus
- Samaritan Man 1
- Samaritan Man 2
- John
- James
- Peter
- Zazab
- Sadducee 1
- Sadducee 2

Costume Trunk Items

A lectionary or Bible, robes, headdresses, veils, shawls, a jug, a tablecloth, a folded goatskin bottle, a cord, a small leather bucket, tables, a bullwhip, coins, and a scroll

Presentation of the Drama
(See resource intro–A, "Leader's Tasks.")

Script for the Background Reading

Catechist. Since the time of Solomon, the Israelites of the north and the Judeans of the south had been separated by prejudice, hatred, and fear. According to the Judeans, the northern people of Galilee were a bunch of low-class peasants. But it was the Samaritans of the central territories who were really the object of racism, discrimination, and religious hatred—who bore the brunt of myriad jokes and were demeaned as impure pigs.

The Samaritans were the lowest of the low in social class. And the most dejected and suspect of these people were the women, considered harborers of lust and seduction. Prejudice breeds injustice, and injustice leads to hatred. A Samaritan woman was not likely to be approached by any law-abiding member of the Jewish faithful. In fact, a good Jewish woman of that era would have considered it a sin to sit down and talk with a Samaritan woman, or even to make eye contact with her. And it was scandalous for a good Jewish man to speak with a Samaritan woman. Yet Jesus approached a Samaritan woman at a well and asked if she would serve him. It was a simple request, this invitation to serve Jesus. It is an invitation that extends to us today.

Meeting Jesus on a hot summer's day beside the ancient well of Jacob healed the abuse of a lifetime, empowering the wounded woman of Samaria to accept herself as a precious child of God. It was to this Samaritan woman that Jesus first revealed his mission as Messiah. It was this woman who first received Jesus' offer of himself as Living Water to the Gentiles. And it was this woman who first proclaimed the Gospel to the people outside of Israel.

Script for the Gospel Reading

[The lector leads everyone in prayer while holding up a lectionary or Bible for all to see.]

Lector. Jesus, Living Water, pour your sacred life into our hearts. You are the deep water that nourishes our spirits. Meet us at the well . . .

[The lector proclaims the Gospel reading for cycle A or B from the lectionary or Bible. Upon finishing, the lector leads the group in response to the Gospel, again holding up the lectionary or Bible for all to see.]

Lector. The Gospel of our Lord Jesus Christ.

Group. Thanks be to God.

Script for the Gospel Drama

[The catechist announces to the group the title of the Gospel scene to be dramatized.]

Catechist. "And the Walls Came Tumbling Down"

[The catechist describes the Gospel scene to the group.]

Catechist. Jesus and his disciples are traveling through Samaria when they come to a fork in the road near the village of Sychar, at the ancient well of Jacob. Jesus, weary and thirsty in the hot Judean desert sun, sits down at the well to rest from the journey. The disciples leave him there and go into the town to find food.

This is our first key to the radical nature of the story we're about to hear. The Jewish rabbis of the day taught that no man dared eat the bread of the foreigners of Samaria. In Sirach 50:25–26 we find that even God's soul is troubled by the nation that sits on the mountain of Samaria.

The disciples have been listening to Jesus' teachings as they travel through Samaria. Although the evangelist John who tells this memory does not mention the nature of Jesus' words on the road to Sychar, we can see their results. Something profoundly life-changing has already happened to these men. Before the story even begins, they have abandoned centuries-old prejudices to follow Jesus in a new way of being people of God. The walls between cultures are being torn down by the love of Christ.

In the heat of the midmorning sun, a Samaritan woman comes to draw water from the well where Jesus sits. The Gospel does not give us her name or fill in the details of her life. But she had a life. She woke up in the morning, she had hopes, fears, and desires in her heart. She was a Samaritan woman, considered a moral outcast by the Jews. What questions about life did she bring with her to the well? We will never know exactly, but we do know that she was an ordinary person with worries and struggles, just like human beings everywhere.

The Gospel this Sunday allows us to listen in on Jesus' private conversation with an ordinary woman as she unburdens her soul to the Christ. The encounter with Jesus makes the woman's heart overflow with so much emotion and joy that she cannot contain it. When a person meets Jesus and permits him to touch her or his life, the result is always new birth.

Samaritan Woman. Midmorning, and the sun is blazing on my back already! Joab?! Are you up yet? I need a little bit of help. I took the heaviest earthen jug we have to the well today and filled it to the brim. I can't manage it another step. Today is going to be another scorcher.

Joab. Just set it down in the doorway. I'll try to carry it in after I finish the last of your artichoke stew. Bring me a drink, woman. Did you hear me? Bring me a drink!

Samaritan Woman. So much for the big, burly watchman at the market-place; . . . at home you're best at lifting a spoon and a cup!

Joab. Your temper rises with the sun, woman. I'm leaving for work so I can get a little peace and quiet. Woman, hold your tongue. I really don't want to hear it! I'm late.

Samaritan Woman. Hold it, Joab! Watch your . . . step.

Joab. Oh! My foot! You put your jug right in my way. Right underfoot in the doorway. I know, I know, you asked me to move it inside, not move it on its side. The jar's clay is cracked now. Oh, well! Make a new one.

Samaritan Woman. Forget the clay. What about my water?!

Joab. You're in luck. There's still some left in the bottom of the jug. But get some more. It's boiling hot in the shade. Have a good day.

Samaritan Woman. Have a good day?! For the love of Bathsheba, I'll never know what binds me to this man!

Catechist. A neighbor woman appears at the Samaritan woman's doorway. She is curious about the morning's commotion.

Ruth the Neighbor. The whole neighborhood will hear you if you shout any louder. What is on your mind?

Samaritan Woman. Come in! Sit! Oh, Ruth, I can't begin to tell you how frustrated I am with my life. The chores are endless. And my Joab is no help. You know how the man is—always hungry, always messing up my house. Just look at how he leaves his robes in a heap beside the bed! And that tablecloth! I scrubbed that cloth clean only yesterday. Now look! Fresh wine stains—purple on the linen. No choice but to go back to the well.

Ruth. I would join you, but I've been up the hill for water twice today already. Wouldn't it be nice if the well were closer to home?

Catechist. Water is precious in an arid land. The woman of Samaria walks to the well at the crossroads of the village, where Jesus is waiting for the disciples to return. Because her large clay jar is cracked, she has brought a folded goatskin bottle, a coil of cord, and a small leather bucket. She unfolds the bottle, loosens the cord, attaches the cord to the bucket, and lowers the bucket deep into the water.

Samaritan Woman. *[To herself]* Hmmmm. Not a woman at the well . . . just a man. Not a bad-looking man. But he's a Jew, not a Samaritan. I'll get my water and leave.

Catechist. Slowly the water fills the bucket and she draws it up. Once the bucket is in her hands, she drinks deeply and then begins to fill her goatskin bottle.

Samaritan Woman. *[Still to herself]* Such a sweltering day. I would have liked to share in a little gossip with the women, but they don't live with Joab. They drew their water in the cool of the day. Only a fool would be out in this heat. And I am a fool for that man!

Speaking of men. I've never seen this one before. A good-looking man . . . though a little dusty around the feet and hem of his robe. I'll just arch this fair old body gracefully over the well, pretend not to see him, and dip my bucket deep into the coolness below once more. I'll bat my eyes quietly and be gone. A minor silent flirtation to spice my day.

Catechist. She begins the ritual of drawing water a second time. But the woman at the well is thirsting for more. With the bucket balanced on one shoulder and her bottle under the other arm, she starts to return home.

Jesus. Woman, would you bring me water?

Samaritan Woman. You're a bold one . . . A Jew, asking *me*, a *Samaritan*, for a drink? Why should I serve you? . . . Why should you ask?

Catechist. The law concerning the behavior of a rabbi is very strict. A rabbi is forbidden to speak to his wife, daughter, or sister in public for fear of devastating his reputation—and yet Rabbi Jesus speaks to this woman of notorious character, a woman of Samaria.

Samaritan Woman. An obvious come-on. You can't ask me, a Samaritan woman, to give you, a Jew, a drink! Jews have nothing in common with Samaritans.

Jesus. If you only knew the gift that God wants to give you, woman. If you knew who I am, you would have asked me to give you Living Water. Anyone who drinks of this water will never be thirsty again.

Samaritan Woman. Blasphemy! This well is over 120 feet deep. You need a bucket to get water out of it. You have no bucket, sir. How could you *get* this Living Water? My ancestor Jacob had to dig this well to find water. There is no living stream here. Are you more powerful than Jacob?

Catechist. This well has a history. It was bought by Jacob and on his deathbed given to Joseph. At the time of the Hebrew Exodus from Egypt, Joseph's body was taken back to Palestine and buried there. This is an appropriate place for Jesus to teach his Gospel.

Samaritan Woman. Let me see if I get this right: Whoever drinks my water will get thirsty again. But anyone who drinks your water—this Living Water, you call it—will never be thirsty anymore . . . Ooh, sounds good to me.

Jesus. The water that I give will become a spring of water gushing up to eternal life.

Samaritan Woman. Sir, give me this water, so that I may never be thirsty or have to keep coming here to draw water.

Jesus. Go, call your husband, and come back.

Samaritan Woman. Go, call my husband? I have no husband.

Jesus. I know. You've had five husbands, but the man you live with now is not your husband.

Catechist. At first hearing we may be tempted to think that Jesus is referring only to this woman's lifestyle, but that is not so. The history of the people of Samaria includes exile and invasion. The Book of Second Kings explains that five groups of people came to take over the land and establish their religions with five foreign gods. Jesus not only speaks to the woman about her five husbands, but addresses Samaria and the five gods to whom the Samaritans have offered their marital commitment of worship.

The Gospel is the inspired Word of God. As such it can teach many lessons, on many levels at the same time. The Gospel stories can address several meanings. On the personal level, the story of the woman at the well is an invitation to repentance. On the corporate level, it is an invitation for the people of Samaria to heal their ancient idolatry.

Samaritan Woman. I see that you are a prophet. Alright, it's true—I'm living with a man who is not my husband. What of it? I'm not a Jew. We don't live by your rules.

No—it's not a perfect relationship. You're right. Sometimes it does hurt—when he doesn't come home, or when he calls on other women. Used? I guess I do feel used.

Jesus. The prophet Isaiah promised the Chosen People that God's children would draw water with joy from the wells of salvation. I will quench the thirst I see in your soul with Living Water.

Samaritan Woman. As if I were a child of God? I thought only Jews were children of God.

Catechist. The people of Samaria are the children of Jacob, but they have intermarried with foreigners, and according to Jewish Law, they are guilty of the unforgivable crime of racial impurity. In this culture if your daughter marries a foreigner, a funeral service is held, for she is considered dead. The woman at the well is a daughter of the ten lost tribes of Israel. According to the prejudice of the day, she and all mixed-blood peoples have lost their Jewish heritage and have no right to share in the blessings of the Covenant. This bitter hatred between peoples has gone on for centuries.

Jesus. Woman, like the ancient psalmist, I see that your soul is thirsty for the living God. The Father has promised to pour water on this thirsty land. I invite you to drink freely from the fountain of Living Water, from the River of Life, from the Water that springs forth from Jerusalem.

Samaritan Woman. Sir, our ancestors worshiped on this mountain, but you Jews say that the place where people must worship is in Jerusalem.

Jesus. Woman, the hour is coming when you will worship the Father neither on this mountain nor in Jerusalem. There is no point entering into the ancient religious arguments that have kept our people apart. Salvation is from the Jews. But the hour is coming, and is now here, when the true worshipers will worship the Father in spirit and truth, for the Father longs for this. God is Spirit, and those who worship God must worship in spirit and truth. I offer you the Spirit of God, Living Water, to satisfy the thirst of your soul. As the prophet Jeremiah taught, the Lord is the fountain of Living Water.

Samaritan Woman. Alright, I'll listen. I know that Messiah is coming, the one called Christ. When he comes, he will proclaim all things to us.

Jesus. I am he, the one who is speaking to you.

Catechist. At this point the disciples return. They are astonished that Jesus is speaking with a woman, but they say nothing. The woman leaves her bucket and goes back to the village, where she meets several people.

Samaritan Woman. *[To the villagers she encounters]* Come and see a man who told me everything I have ever done! Could he be the One, the Messiah?

Catechist. Many Samaritans become followers of the Christ because of her testimony. The Gospel says Jesus stays in Samaria two days. And many more believe because of his word.

Samaritan Man 1. Woman, we believe what you said about Jesus. Now we have heard for ourselves.

Samaritan Man 2. We know that Jesus is truly the Savior of the world.

Catechist. The Gospel passage on the Samaritan woman focuses on the catechumenal and baptismal dimensions of Lent. It invites us to appreciate our own encounter with the Lord in prayer, to hear what Jesus is telling us about our own life, and to reach out for the gift of Living Water.

Our drama continues as we consider the third Sunday of Lent's Gospel in cycle B—a liturgy of the word calling us to justice through the story of the cleansing of the Temple . . .

The Passover is near, so Jesus and his disciples leave Jacob's well and continue on their journey to Jerusalem. When Jesus arrives at the Temple, he finds people selling cattle, sheep, and doves, and money changers seated at their tables in the Temple courtyard. Making a whip of cords, he drives all of the people and their animals out. He spills the money changers' coins on the floor and throws over the tables.

Jesus. Take these things out of here! Stop making my Father's house a marketplace!

John. What is Jesus doing? We're all going to be arrested.

James. The Sadducees are going to have a fit.

Peter. Remember the Scriptures' prophecy that Messiah will be consumed with zeal for the house of God.

Zazab. *[Running out of the Temple and meeting two Sadducees]* Who does this Jesus think he is? He's going to ruin the baker's business. Did you hear what he just did? He got his nose twisted out of joint just because we were selling a few trinkets in the Temple courtyard. He got this bullwhip and went running through the courtyard, tearing up the stands and displays; laid Zorba's aphrodisiac stand to waste—totaled it, totaled it! He was screaming his head off!

Jesus. *[From inside the Temple]* My Father's house—my Temple—should be a house of prayer. You've made it into a den of thieves! Get out! Get out!

Zazab. This Jesus has no respect for a businessman's profit margin.

Sadducee 1. Well, we will speak to this zealous Rabbi. We will see what he has to say about himself.

[Zazab and the two Sadducees go into the Temple to find Jesus.]

Sadducee 2. Jesus, your disciples speak as if you are the promised Messiah. So are you? Yes? What sign can you give us?

Jesus. Destroy this temple, and in three days I will raise it up.

Zazab. See, I told you. He really has it in for the Temple.

Sadducee 2. It has been forty-six years since Herod began the reconstruction of this ancient Temple. Will you raise it up in three days?

Sadducees 1 and 2 and Zazab. Ha! Ha! Ha! *[Laughing their heads off]*

Catechist. Jesus is actually speaking of the temple of his body. Later, after he is raised from the dead, his disciples will remember this prophecy of the Resurrection.

    Jesus doesn't care about being accepted by the established powers of his time. His publicly accepting the worth of the Samaritan woman and cleansing the Temple make enemies of the Sadducees and the disciples of Jesus. From that time on, the Sanhedrin (the supreme council and tribunal of the Jews) says that Jesus is causing seditious agitation, that he is a troublemaker who is rousing the population. They watch and wait for Jesus to fall into their hands.

Follow-up After the Drama

(See resource intro–A, "Leader's Tasks.")

Reflection Questions

- Who are the alienated and prejudiced people in our culture? How does the story of Jesus and the Samaritan woman challenge our world's bigotry?
- What does Jesus' encounter with the Samaritan woman say to our churches, our political parties, our cities, and our families?
- What would you have thought if you had seen Jesus with a bullwhip at the Temple?
- How can our passion for buying and selling sometimes block our relationship with God?
- How are our bodies God's temple? What does that teaching from Jesus tell us about God's expectations of our behaviors and choices?

Improv

(See resource intro–A, "Leader's Tasks.")

Closure

(See resource intro–A, "Leader's Tasks.")

Illustration by Vicki Shuck

Fourth Sunday of Lent Icon

When we see through the eyes of Jesus, we understand that eternal life is more than life after death—it is living God's love now and forever. A: John, chapter 9; B: John 3:14–21; C: Luke 15:1–32. This drama focuses on the readings for cycles A and B.

Fourth Sunday of Lent

The readings for the three cycles of this Sunday are so rich that we could not combine them into a single drama. This drama reflects only the Gospel stories from cycles A and B of the lectionary. Note that if your parish has an RCIA program, this is a scrutiny Sunday. The scrutinies always use the cycle A readings.

Gospel Readings and Themes

Cycle A. John, chapter 9. Healing of the blind: the Light of the World.
Cycle B. John 3:14–21. Believing offers eternal life.

Preparation for the Drama
(See resource intro–A, "Leader's Tasks.")

Roles

Catechist, who coordinates the drama
Lector, who leads the opening prayer and proclaims the sacred Scriptures
Gospel players, who enflesh the roles in the scriptural drama

- Jesus
- Man in the Crowd
- Woman in the Crowd
- Child in the Crowd
- Bartimaeus the Man Born Blind
- Elderly Man
- Merchant
- Teenager in the Crowd
- James
- Peter
- Martha of Bethany
- Antonius
- Matthew
- Axis
- John
- Man 1
- Man 2
- Woman 1
- Woman 2
- Pharisee 1
- Pharisee 2
- Pharisee 3
- Judith
- Esdras

Costume Trunk Items

A lectionary or Bible, robes, headdresses, veils, and sacks of junk (for Bartimaeus)

Presentation of the Drama
(See resource intro–A, "Leader's Tasks.")

Script for the Background Reading

Catechist. All of us begin our walk in blindness. Like the man born blind in John's Gospel, we too are sent to the pool of Siloam to wash away our resentments, our prejudices, our bigotry, and our fear so that we can become what God created us to be, worthy to call ourselves followers of Christ. The only Jesus that many will meet in their lives is the Christ we carry in our hearts. We, the disciples of Jesus, are the students of the Great Teacher. Pray that we learn the truths of the Gospel well.

The story of Bartimaeus uses several plays on words. The word *apostle* means "one sent," and Jesus sends his Apostles to proclaim the Good News. The man born blind is sent to the pool of Siloam, and the word *Siloam* itself means "sent." We are the Apostles and the blind man. We are the vessels Christ sends to offer light in the darkness, healing to the suffering.

The Gospel of Jesus has no other human means to be proclaimed to the ends of the earth but through our flesh. Our lives are the witness of God's love to the world. Our challenge during this Lent is to remove the blindness from our own souls, so as to be worthy vessels of the Good News for others.

Script for the Gospel Reading

[The lector leads everyone in prayer while holding up a lectionary or Bible for all to see.]

Lector. Creator God, open our eyes. Help us to recognize the things in our lives that keep us in spiritual blindness. Jesus, Lord of life, teach us to seek the light, the truth, the way of love. Transform us into people who cherish justice, mercy, and compassion. Strengthen us to see with your eyes and to offer ourselves as your hands to build a world where God's will is done on earth as it is in heaven.

[The lector proclaims the Gospel reading for cycle A or B from the lectionary or Bible. Upon finishing, the lector leads the group in response to the Gospel, again holding up the lectionary or Bible for all to see.]

Lector. The Gospel of our Lord Jesus Christ.

Group. Thanks be to God.

Script for the Gospel Drama

[The catechist announces to the group the title of the Gospel scene to be dramatized.]

Catechist. "Against All Odds"

[The catechist describes the Gospel scene to the group.]

Catechist. In the time of Jesus, people believed that those who were poor, sick, crippled, and mentally ill were personally responsible for their condition. Possibly they or their parents had committed a sin that caused the affliction. Sickness was thought to be a punishment from God. Still today there are those who think that. Even though the Gospel for this Sunday clearly denies that God sends disease, some refuse to be compassionate toward those who are sick and instead condemn them as sinners.

In today's Gospel Jesus and a number of disciples come upon a man who has been blind from birth. Everyone in the village knows this man. When asked who is responsible for his blindness, the man or his parents, Jesus clearly says "Neither!" Jesus reminds his disciples then and now that the full meaning of human suffering has not been revealed. We have control over some of the situations in our lives, but others remain in the realm of mystery. Wisdom is knowing the difference.

This man born blind is the only person in the Gospel stories who is identified as one with an affliction from birth. Jesus' touch gives him his sight. His healing changes the way the whole community understands the will of God. How important is this lesson? So important that we still contemplate its wisdom two thousand years later.

[Jesus makes his way through a crowd of villagers.]

Man in the Crowd. He's coming! Here he comes! Look how he works a crowd wherever he goes! I think I see someone fainting in his presence! I would like to see him up close, just once.

Woman in the Crowd. In this mob? Forget it. You have to be superspecial or something. Like those groupies who hang at his feet wherever he goes.

Child in the Crowd. Miracles happen, ya know? I saw him cure a little girl once, who was very sick. I'm not kidding. This guy's a healer. He's cured thousands.

Man in the Crowd. Well, good luck! Looks like he's leaving. Eat his dust if you like. I know better than to believe in something I can't see with my own eyes!

Bartimaeus the Man Born Blind. Is it really *the* Jesus of Nazareth? Is it him? Please, tell me, someone! Is it the one called Jesus?

Child in the Crowd. Yes! You can almost hear his voice now if you try hard. He's coming this way, passing us by.

Bartimaeus. Jesus, Son of David, have pity on me!

Man in the Crowd. These street people really irritate me. Quiet, fool! Jesus is on his way out of town. This gathering is history. You missed your chance. He especially doesn't have time for blind, begging fools!

Bartimaeus. Jesus, Son of David, have pity on me!

Woman in the Crowd. He's too blind to see how ridiculous he is—like Jesus would listen to *him!*

Elderly Man. Please contain yourself, Bartimaeus, and stop humiliating yourself. This outburst is such low-class behavior. Your yelling is a big bother. It's getting you nowhere and it's an embarrassment to us! Quiet! Quiet! Quiet!

Merchant. You bum! You boring bag man! Take your sacks of junk and get out of here!

Teenager in the Crowd. Yeah! Take your junk and leave!

Catechist. The problem of suffering has always mystified humanity. If God loves us, why does suffering exist? The disciples in this Gospel story were people of their time. In their culture, suffering was always thought to be connected to sin. The disciples assumed that wherever there was suffering, there was sin. In a sense this was (and is) true, but the sin may not be the personal sin of the person who carries the burden. Pope John Paul II has asked Christians to be aware that there are two kinds of sin: personal and corporate. There is the sin you and I commit when we choose to be cruel or selfish, and there are sinful structures that a society or group permits. We measure ourselves and our communities by the way we and our systems are set up to treat and care for others.

Walking along the dusty paths with the Christ, the disciples in our story come upon the blind man Bartimaeus begging by the roadside. They ask Jesus this question:

James. Rabbi, why was this man born blind?

Peter. Who is guilty of the sin? Is it this blind man sitting by the side of the road? or his parents?

James. Is his blindness due to his own sin? Perhaps a hidden guilt imprisons him?

Martha of Bethany. I heard he's been blind from birth. Babies can't commit sin. Children are innocent of any wrongdoing. His blindness is from some other cause.

Peter. Some teach that a person begins to sin while still in the mother's womb.

Martha. How could that be, Peter? Nothing is more precious and pure than a baby.

Catechist. A crowd starts to gather around Jesus and the disciples, as it always does whenever Jesus begins to teach. A Greek hears the conversation and adds:

Antonius. From the formation of the embryo in the womb, evil influences a person.

Matthew. If the evil impulse began with the formation of the embryo, then the child would kick in the womb and break his or her way out.

Martha. It surely can feel like a child in the womb wants to kick its way out! *[She laughs.]* Sorry, you men wouldn't understand.

Axis. All souls before conception are good; it is their entry into the body that contaminates them. The spirit is holy. The flesh is evil.

Peter. Lord, are these Greeks right? Is that why the man is blind? Was he contaminated by the flesh, or is he blind because of sin?

Catechist. People in the time of Jesus believed that everything was infected by sin. It was almost as if sin was a creature, a parasite, a demon that like a vampire wanted to enter the world. The people were onto something. But they were asking the wrong questions. They were observing something about how the world works, without the knowledge of biology and ecology to properly understand it. Now we know that if parents have a defective gene, it may be passed on to a child. We know that if a parent has a virus, a child may contract the infection.

Jesus' culture turned its back on the sick, assuming that some infraction of God's law justified their unfortunate conditions. Lepers were abandoned, the lame cast off, and the blind condemned. The people thought not only that the sin of parents could be transferred to their baby, causing birth defects, but that an affliction like blindness was the result of sin committed even before birth, by an embryo.

John. The Scriptures teach us that God feels strongly about sin.

Peter. Exodus says that God is a jealous God, visiting the iniquity of the fathers upon even great-great-grandchildren.

Jesus. It is not God who passes on the suffering. Most times, suffering is the result of human choice. The consequences of sin pass through the generations, but it is not God who has created or willed this suffering.

John. This man has not chosen his blindness. His blindness has nothing to do with his will. Answer clearly, Rabbi: Who sinned, this blind man or his parents? Who has sinned?

Jesus. Neither! There are many reasons for suffering, but my heavenly Father never punishes children for the sins of their parents.

James. The Psalms say, "May the iniquity of his father be remembered before the LORD, / and do not let the sin of his mother be blotted out."

Jesus. The psalmist felt angry. I commend the author for not exacting revenge, for leaving the final outcome to God. But the God of Israel is the God of mercy. Wrath means experiencing the logical outcome of our choices.

Martha. Some say God's wrath is eternal. If the parents sinned, then God never forgets the wrong. The punishment is inevitable. Is this true, Jesus?

Jesus. What kind of God would that be? My Father is love and life, not revenge and prejudice. God is compassion. God is mercy. My Father so loves the world that he gave his only Son, so that everyone who believes in him may not perish but may have eternal life.

Bartimaeus. Jesus, Son of David, have pity on me!

Jesus. Please, push aside and make way for him . . . Sir, I hear you calling me. What do you want me to do for you?

Bartimaeus. Master, I want to see!

Peter. Why, Lord, must this man live his life in blindness?

Jesus. This man's affliction will transform into joy. God's grace will be revealed so as to build your faith. Now is the time. I must do the work of the Father while it is day. As long as I am in the world, I am the Light of the World.

Catechist. When he has said this, he spits on the ground and makes mud with the saliva and spreads the mud on the man's eyes. Jesus speaks to the blind man:

Jesus. Go, wash in the pool of Siloam.

Catechist. Jesus speaks to the people in a language and a symbol that they understand. The use of spittle to heal is common in their world. The spittle of a sacred person is a powerful tool to ward off sickness, especially as protection against being cursed by the evil eye. Jesus smears spit and mud on the man's eyes, and the man can see! The people in the neighborhood doubt this truth even though it is right before their eyes. The blind becomes sighted, and the sighted cannot believe what their eyes are seeing.

[Back in the village]

Man 1. Isn't that Bartimaeus the beggar?

Man 2. Isn't he the blind man? He sees. What happened here?

Woman 1. No, he looks like him, but it can't be him. . . .

Woman 2. No, it can't be him.

Bartimaeus. I am the man. I am Bartimaeus the blind man, and I can see!

Man 1. How were your eyes opened?

Man 2. How can a man blind from birth . . . see? You see me, don't you? He sees!

Bartimaeus. The man called Jesus made mud with his spittle, spread it on my eyes, and said to me, "Go to Siloam and wash." I did as Jesus told me, and—praise God—I see! For the love of God, rejoice!

Jesus. You will have the gift of sight because of your great trust in me. Go your way; your faith has saved you.

Pharisee 1. So this Jesus heals on the Sabbath? Is he above the Law? How dare he!

Pharisee 2. A man may not fill a dish with oil, or put a wick in it, without breaking the law of Sabbath.

Pharisee 3. A man cannot cut his fingernails or pull out a hair of his head or his beard without breaking the Sabbath law. Thou shalt not work on Sabbath! It is the Law!

Pharisee 1. *[To Bartimaeus]* Who is this Jesus who breaks the Sabbath? Who dares to work on the Sabbath? Your life was not in actual danger; he didn't *need* to do this today.

Pharisee 2. Placing "fasting spittle" upon the eyelids is not lawful on the Sabbath. It is written! It is forbidden! Does this Jesus mock the Law of Moses?!

Catechist. There are those in every generation who condemn anyone whose ideas are different from their own. They see themselves as the authority before God, and reject anyone with new or different ideas. They think that their way of honoring God is the only way. Jesus stood firm against the critics of his day. To Jesus, the person was always more important than self-righteous legalism.

Pharisee 1. Where is he? Where is this Jesus who heals on the Sabbath?

Bartimaeus. I do not know!

Pharisee 2. Bartimaeus! How did you receive your sight?

Bartimaeus. Jesus called to me, and put mud on my eyes. I washed, and now I see.

Pharisee 1. Jesus made the mud and opened your eyes?! On the Sabbath?! He heals on the Lord's Day?! He does not observe the Sabbath! This Jesus is evil. He is not from God!

Pharisee 3. But, Brother, he must be from God! How can a man who is a sinner perform such signs? How can anyone do such works and not be of God?! We mustn't forget that Moses proved that he really was God's messenger, by the signs and wonders that he performed. Elijah proved that he was a genuine prophet by doing things the prophets of Baal could not do. Are you sure you want to condemn this Jesus, Brother?

Pharisee 2. You're such a liberal! You're as bad as these fools. Anyone who starts talking about this Jesus like he is the Messiah will be put out of the synagogue. Do you all hear me?! So, Bartimaeus, what do you think of this Nazarene? How did you regain your sight? Who is this Jesus?

Bartimaeus. He is a prophet of God. He touched me, and now I see. I was blind, and now I see. That's all I know. Jesus healed me.

Pharisee 1. You're a fraud! You haven't been blind from birth. This is all an act to get followers for this new rabbi. Confess, and it will go easier on you, liar!

Pharisee 2. Is this your son, woman?

Judith. Yes. This is Bartimaeus.

Esdras. This is our son . . . Why do you ask?

Pharisee 2. Do you verify that he was born blind?

Pharisee 3. How has he been healed? It is clear that he is no longer blind!

Judith. We know that this is our son, and that he was born blind . . .

Esdras. Stop frightening my wife. All we know is that now he sees. We thank God our son has been healed. *How* he has been healed is a mystery to us.

Judith. We do not know who opened his eyes . . . We are as surprised as you are. . . .

Esdras. Ask him. He is old enough to speak for himself.

Catechist. These parents seem less than supportive of their son, but there is a cultural explanation for their behavior. The authorities of this time have a great deal of power over the population. They have the power of the *cherem*, by which one is banished from the synagogue, publicly shamed, and cursed. It is an excommunication that inflicts terror, removing the support of the community and of God. Sometimes the sentence is temporary; sometimes it is for life.

Pharisee 1. You should give glory only to God! Jesus is a sinner like the rest of you.

Bartimaeus. Please do not terrify my aged parents. I am old enough to speak for myself. I do not know whether Jesus is a sinner. One thing I do know is that I was blind, and now I see. I thank the Lord for this gift.

Pharisee 3. What did he do to you? How did he open your eyes?

Bartimaeus. I have told you already, and you would not listen. Why do you want to hear it again? Do you also want to become his disciples?

Pharisee 1. You are his disciple. We are disciples of Moses. We know that God has spoken to Moses, but as for this man, we do not know where he comes from. Who are you, Jesus? Are you a prophet? or the son of a serpent?

Jesus. And just as Moses lifted up the serpent in the wilderness, so must the Son of God be lifted up, that whoever believes in him may have eternal life.

Bartimaeus. That's astonishing! You don't know where he comes from, yet he gave me back my sight. Brothers, I can see. Since the beginning of the world, never have we heard of anyone who could heal the eyes of the blind with a touch. If Jesus were not from God, he could do nothing.

Pharisee 1. I am a Pharisee! A doctor of the Law! You were born entirely in sin, and are you trying to teach us? Who do you think you are, Beggar?!

Catechist. And they drive the man who was born blind, the man who can now see, from their midst. Jesus searches for him, and the Pharisees follow. When Jesus finds Bartimaeus, he asks him:

Jesus. Bartimaeus, do you believe in the Son of God?

Bartimaeus. And who is he, sir? Tell me, so that I may believe in him.

Jesus. Your eyes, which were once blind, now see him. I am he.

Bartimaeus. Lord Jesus, I believe in you.

Jesus. I came into this world . . . so that those who do not see may see, and those who do see may become blind.

Pharisee 3. Surely we are not blind, are we?

Jesus. Those who are blind are innocent of any sin. But you are fully responsible for your ignorance. You have the gift of sight, and yet you refuse to see. Your pride blinds you to the truth. Your sin remains.

Pharisee 1. Are you the judge, Jesus?!

Jesus. This is the judgment; the Light has come into the world. Those who love darkness rather than Light do so because evil is uncomfortable in the Light. The Light exposes evil deeds. Those who live in Truth love the Light. They are in God.

Pharisee 1. Are you condemning us, Jesus?!

Jesus. Indeed, God did not send the Son into the world to condemn the world, but in order that the world might be saved through him. Those who believe in him are not condemned; but those who do not believe are condemned already, because they have not believed in the name of the only Son of God.

Catechist. The turning point of this story is one person's faith. Jesus often spoke of the power of such faith—"If you have faith the size of a mustard seed, it will yield a mighty tree" . . . "Faith moves mountains" . . . "Ask and you shall receive" . . . "Blessed is the one who has believed and not seen." When the blind man's persistence and deep faith result in a miraculous healing of his sight, the spiritual eyes of those around him are opened too.

Jesus wants to love us, to offer us freedom from our blindness, to offer us a more full life, beginning now and lasting into eternity. Jesus offers liberty to captives, sight to those who are blind, and the gift of eternal life. Jesus offers salvation and freedom to all of us regardless of our status, class, creed, race, or gender . . . All of us are children of the loving God of compassion.

Follow-up After the Drama
(See resource intro–A, "Leader's Tasks.")

Reflection Questions

- To Jesus, the blind beggar was worthy of attention and respect. Can you think of a moment when prejudice blinded you to the truth of someone's dignity? How can we show attention and respect to those who are shunned in some way by the crowd?
- Had the blind man listened to the crowd, he wouldn't have gotten the gift God offered him. Can you think of parallel situations—when "following the crowd" might mean losing out on gifts God has in store for you?
- The blind man had a problem that everyone could see. Some handicaps are more hidden. All of us face challenges as we live day to day. What does the blind man's story teach us about risking and reaching out for help?
- When you look at yourself through the eyes of Christ, can you recognize your own blindness? What areas of darkness would you ask Christ to heal? How do those areas affect your relationship with Jesus? with others?
- When looking toward Jesus, we see the way to God. How does Christ ask us to live more intentional Christian lives? How does Christ challenge us to live in the truth, in the light?

Improv
(See resource intro–A, "Leader's Tasks.")

Closure
(See resource intro–A, "Leader's Tasks.")

Illustration by Vicki Shuck

Fifth Sunday of Lent Icon

Jesus shows us that God is compassion and mercy, a God of life! It's no surprise, then, that when we face difficult times, God brings us to new life. A: John 11:1–45; B: John 12:20–33; C: John 8:1–11. This drama focuses on the readings for cycles A and B.

Fifth Sunday of Lent

The readings for the three cycles of this Sunday are so rich that we could not combine them into a single drama. This drama reflects only the Gospel stories from cycles A and B of the lectionary. Note that if your parish has an RCIA program, this is a scrutiny Sunday. The scrutinies always use the cycle A readings.

Gospel Readings and Themes

Cycle A. John 11:1–45. The resurrection of Lazarus.
Cycle B. John 12:20–33. We want to see Jesus.

Preparation for the Drama
(See resource intro–A, "Leader's Tasks.")

Roles

Catechist, who coordinates the drama
Lector, who leads the opening prayer and proclaims the sacred Scriptures
Gospel players, who enflesh the roles in the scriptural drama
- Aunt Miriam
- Elisheva the Family Friend
- Martha of Bethany
- Davida the Skeptic
- Mary of Bethany
- Jesus
- John
- Thomas
- Lazarus
- Demetri
- Nicos
- Philip
- Andrew
- Voice from Heaven

Costume Trunk Items

A lectionary or Bible, robes, headdresses, veils, something to represent the stone in front of Lazarus's tomb, and a long cotton or linen "burial cloth" to cover Lazarus

Presentation of the Drama

(See resource intro–A, "Leader's Tasks.")

Script for the Background Reading

Catechist. Of all the many miracles Christ performed as he walked upon this earth, none speaks to us more profoundly than the raising of Lazarus. God calls each of us—like Lazarus—out of our own "sleep" and breathes new life into our spirit if we but seek Jesus.

The amazing story of the resurrection of Lazarus testifies to the fullness of Christ's divinity. Only almighty God can take death and turn it to life. For many at the time, undoubtedly, the raising of Lazarus revealed Christ's true identity, shattering all doubts and instilling unwavering faith. In this miracle, Jesus also foreshadowed his own death and burial and resurrected glory—his ultimate victory over all death forever.

This Gospel story leaves us feeling in awe of Jesus, and yet closer to him, because he is just as human as he is divine. Jesus loved deeply, and was attached to the people he loved. He did not want to lose Lazarus; arriving in Bethany, he stood near the grave of his close friend and could not even speak. Suffering terrible sadness, *Jesus wept.* It is awesome to recognize that Jesus, who is truly divine and truly human, was deeply emotional and passionately loved his friends.

The second Gospel reading for this Sunday, for cycle B, also dwells on death. Death is a part of life that no one will escape, and with it comes grief and sadness. In the second reading, Jesus reveals the fear and anguish that threaten to overwhelm him as he faces his own looming death. In both readings, the story does not end with death. Mysteriously and miraculously, against all odds, death turns to life. These events speak to the very heart of our Catholic Christian faith.

Script for the Gospel Reading

[The lector leads everyone in prayer while holding up a lectionary or Bible for all to see.]

Lector. Jesus, Lord of life, you whose power can transform the darkest and most hopeless tragedy into glorious rebirth, please fill our hearts with hope. Help us to transform the dark times and challenges we face. We have only to take you at your word. Strengthen our belief, and bring us safely through the years of this life and into life everlasting.

[The lector proclaims the Gospel reading for cycle A or B from the lectionary or Bible. Upon finishing, the lector leads the group in response to the Gospel, again holding up the lectionary or Bible for all to see.]

Lector. The Gospel of our Lord Jesus Christ.

Group. Thanks be to God.

Script for the Gospel Drama

[The catechist announces to the group the title of the Gospel scene to be dramatized.]

Catechist. "Out of the Darkness, into the Light"

[The catechist describes the Gospel scene to the group.]

Catechist. In the following scene, Martha of Bethany and her sister Mary grieve over the death of their brother Lazarus. Martha, Mary, and Lazarus are close friends of Jesus', and the two women are heartsick that Jesus did not reach Bethany in time to heal Lazarus. Relatives and friends gather around them—Aunt Miriam; the kindhearted Elisheva; and Davida, a bossy but well-meaning neighbor—but the sisters are inconsolable.

Aunt Miriam. Martha, I came the minute I heard the news. Can it be true about our dear Lazarus? This seems like a horrible mistake. Why him and not me? He was so young! I am so old!

Elisheva the Family Friend. Yes, it's like a bad dream. This death was far too sudden.

Martha of Bethany. Oh, Elisheva, my heart is broken. Lazarus was healthy and vigorous two weeks ago. When the illness hit that morning after the Sabbath, we sent immediately for Jesus. I believe that if the Master had been with us, Lazarus would still be alive. But Jesus never reached us in time.

Davida the Skeptic. So, where is he, where is he? God knows he's had enough dinners at this house.

Elisheva. Don't you understand, Davida, that the authorities here recently tried to stone him? It's a risk for Jesus to come back to this part of Judea at all.

Davida. I thought you said he was the Messiah. The Messiah should have been able to prevent this. To him it should have been easy.

Mary of Bethany. He *is* the Messiah. There must be a very good reason for his delay. Nevertheless, our brother is dead, and nothing will ever bring him back.

Elisheva. We all loved your brother, Mary, as though he were our own.

Aunt Miriam. We have lost him, and it hurts. But Lazarus lives on in our memory. That is the one thing that death cannot steal!

Catechist. For the faithful Jews who lived at the time that Jesus walked the earth, death meant the final, irreversible separation from life and love. One school of Jewish thought, however, maintained that the deceased went to Sheol, a netherworld of shadows and silence. The afterlife that Jesus' death and Resurrection would make possible—an afterlife filled with joy and meaning—was a gift far beyond what anyone in Jesus' world would have dared dream.

Davida. Martha! Word has come that Jesus is in the area. So, Jesus finally graces the outskirts of our village. Four days too late, but who is counting?!

Catechist. A large gathering of Jews have come to pay their respects to Lazarus. Now the crowd parts so that Jesus and Martha can pass to each other.

Martha. Master! We lost Lazarus because you were not with us. We needed you. Where were you?

Jesus. Martha, I was with you in spirit the whole time.

Martha. Mary and I took turns climbing the hill to see if you were on your way. You were our one hope. But even now I know that God will listen to you and give you whatever you ask. Remember Lazarus, Lord, when you enter into your Reign.

Jesus. Your brother will rise again.

Martha. Of course, Rabbi . . . in the resurrection, on the last day.

Jesus. Martha, I am the Resurrection and the Life. I, Jesus, am the Resurrection and the Life. Whoever believes in me, even though they die, will live. I promise you, Martha, Lazarus will never die. Do you believe this?

Martha. Yes, Lord, I believe you are the Christ, the Son of God, the One who was to come into the world . . . Messiah. My sister Mary also believes. And so did Lazarus. Remember him, Lord.

Catechist. Jesus is the Resurrection and the Life. "Do you believe?" he asks. It's a personal question we must each ask ourselves: "Do I believe? Do I take Jesus at his word?" Ultimately, every one of us must give an answer. Martha's sister Mary believed deeply—so deeply, the Gospel tells us, that she gave Jesus her full attention when he dined in her home.

Mary. Master! We missed you so terribly. One of the last things Lazarus said was, "Tell Jesus that I loved him." He didn't want to leave this earth without the two of you seeing each other one last time. He tried so hard to hold on to life.

Catechist. When we pray for those we love who are ill or hurting or in trouble, sometimes it seems that God is not listening. But just as in the case of Lazarus, God hears every prayer and always has a purpose and a plan.

 Moreover, God grieves with us when we are in pain. On the day he went to Bethany, Jesus was moved in his spirit and he wept.

John. Thomas, have you ever seen such an expression on the Master's face?

Thomas. Tears are in his eyes. He loved Lazarus.

John. I've noticed that the Master feels all the things that we feel . . . sorrow, loneliness, joy, fear. Jesus is powerful, but he is vulnerable too.

Davida. So he's crying? He should be crying! But what are tears? They cost nothing. They change nothing.

Aunt Miriam. His tears tell me that he is moved and feels great love. But something doesn't add up. All the people Jesus has supposedly healed—that blind man who got to see again, and the cripple I heard about who got up and walked? Jesus helps strangers, so why not a friend as loyal as Lazarus?

Jesus. Where have they laid him? Where have they laid my friend?

Mary. Come, Lord, follow us . . .

Catechist. Lazarus has been laid to rest in a common cave, sealed with a large stone so that no one may enter.

Jesus. Take away the stone!

Martha. Good Lord! The smell of decay would overcome you. You mustn't open the tomb. He's been in there for four days!

Jesus. Take away the stone! Trust me, I give you my word . . . On this day, you will see the glory of God.

Davida. He's just kidding, Martha. He's kidding, right? What does Jesus think he's doing? My God, he will be unclean for days.

[The Apostles move the stone.]

Thomas. Look! We have rolled away the stone!

Jesus. Lazarus! Come out!

Aunt Miriam. *[Covering her eyes with her hands]* Oh, this will be horrible. He shouldn't play with our hearts this way.

[Lazarus emerges from the cave, wrapped in a long burial cloth.]

Elisheva. Oh, my God . . . I see him! Miriam, take your hands off your eyes.

Aunt Miriam. It's a ghost! Standing at the mouth of the cave!

Mary. It's my brother, it's my brother . . .

Thomas. HE LIVES!

John. HE LIVES!

Davida. Oh, my God . . . he lives.

Jesus. Unbind the man. Set him free.

Catechist. Jesus has raised his friend from the dead, but he asks the people around Lazarus—the community—to unwind the burial cloth that is wrapped around Lazarus. We are called to unbind one another and set one another free.

Jesus has performed dozens of miracles at this point in his ministry, and has clearly shown himself to be in command of the natural world. But this miracle is so utterly extraordinary, and so clearly divine, that the crowd explodes.

Martha. Lazarus! Brother! You are alive!

Lazarus. Lord, I saw the light, and I walked toward it and the light was you. You are the Light of the World.

Mary. Lord, you are the Resurrection and the Life. I believe in you. Now all the world will believe. You take death and turn it to life.

Catechist. The miracle of the raising of Lazarus reveals the nature of Jesus, who is God incarnate, the giver of all life, the Christ. Like all human beings, Jesus will one day die, but death will not have the last word. The miracle that day in Bethany foreshadows Jesus' own destiny. In fact, his own Resurrection will be even more glorious. Whereas the stone that covered Lazarus's cave, and the burial cloths that bound him, had to be removed by human hands, only the hand of God will open the tomb of the Christ on the first Easter morning. And whereas Lazarus, in time, will die a natural death, Jesus will arise from the grave to live forever—and will call us to follow him into eternal life.

The story of Lazarus spreads across Judea like wildfire. Within days the political crosscurrents swirling around Jesus intensify because of the controversy surrounding this great miracle. Jesus' enemies escalate their plot to destroy him. People from all over Palestine come looking, hoping to see Jesus.

It is the week before Passover, and Jesus is now in Jerusalem. Some Greek travelers have journeyed to Jerusalem to see this Rabbi who has raised a man from the dead.

Demetri. We have come to see the Nazarene who touches people and they are healed. We have heard of his amazing deeds, even raising the dead to life!

Nicos. Just one look. We have heard the stories. Please, we want to see Jesus.

Catechist. These Greeks are among the first seekers who long to find God in the traditions of Judaism. Their desire "to see" Jesus can be translated from the original text to reveal a desire "to believe in" Jesus. They seek entrance to the realm of Jesus through his disciples, just as today one must often try to find Jesus through a disciple, through believers, through the church.

Philip. Andrew, do you think Jesus is too tired? Is this exhausting him?

Andrew. We can ask him. He does look tired.

Philip and Andrew. Lord, visitors are here for the Passover. Can they see you?

Jesus. Friends, welcome them. Teach them to keep seeking truth. My heart is heavy. The hour has arrived for which I came into this world. It will be hard for all of us. But you are not to be afraid . . . Unless a grain of wheat falls into the earth and dies, it will remain just a single grain; but if it does die in the soil, it will bear so much more wheat. Those who love their life will lose it, and those who hate their life in this world will keep it for eternal life.

Philip. Oh, no. Jesus, what are you talking about?

Andrew. They wouldn't kill him, Philip, would they? . . . Jesus, all of us will stand by you. We won't let them hurt you. Never!

Jesus. Philip, Andrew, my friends, we have walked so many miles together, broken bread and offered thanks. You've listened to my stories and told me your own. We know one another. We care for one another. I have to tell you the truth. Tonight my soul is troubled. And I am afraid.

Andrew. We're all afraid, Master. The winds are blowing in all directions at once. These Greeks want to see you, but others in power wish never to lay eyes on you again.

Jesus. I could ask my Father to save me, Andrew, but my whole purpose for coming to this earth is at hand. My mission is to face what God is asking of me, no matter the price. I must glorify my Father's name.

Voice from Heaven. "I have glorified it, and I will glorify it again."

Nicos. What was that? Did you hear something?

Demetri. Thunder. I heard thunder. What did you hear?

Nicos. I heard an angel. An angel blessing the Rabbi from Nazareth.

Philip. Lord, I've heard about the voice from heaven—Peter told us about hearing it that day at the Jordan, the day you were baptized. Is it the same voice?

Jesus. Yes, Philip, and the voice is for you, and Andrew, and the travelers from Greece. It is to help you understand and believe when my hour comes.

Catechist. As Jesus faces the cruelty and agony of his last week on earth, he is in full union, one in spirit, with the Father. Jesus' sacrifice on the cross will fulfill his earthly mission; it will conquer death, so that death is now a doorway through which we all can pass to live with God forever. From the beginning, God loved us and wanted us, and the Incarnation reveals that to us in a personal and powerful way.

One week before Passion Sunday, we prayerfully prepare for the most sacred and solemn days of our liturgical year. As a family of believers, we join hearts and together enter into the mystery and the memory of God's infinitely merciful act of love on the cross, a sacrifice that embraces and saves the whole world.

Follow-up After the Drama
(See resource intro–A, "Leader's Tasks.")

Reflection Questions

- If Jesus can take death and turn it into life, then consider what he can do with all the situations in our lives. How might his life-giving grace transform a difficulty that you are dealing with right now? Have you asked him to help you?
- The two sisters of Lazarus were disappointed that Jesus did not show up when they called for help. But Jesus did show up, and his timing had an important purpose. Do you ever pray for someone you love who is ill or hurting or in trouble? Does it seem sometimes that God is not listening? How does the story of Lazarus shed new light on this?
- Have you ever felt buried under the weight of a particular sin, a foolish mistake, or bad habits? Jesus calls us back to life each time he sets us free with his forgiveness and love. Do you believe this with all your heart?

Improv
(See resource intro–A, "Leader's Tasks.")

Closure
(See resource intro–A, "Leader's Tasks.")

Illustration by Vicki Shuck

Passion Sunday, or Palm Sunday, Icon

Here we have two scenes of Jesus being honored: one, from today's drama, of people celebrating Jesus' arrival in Jerusalem, and the other of Lazarus's sister Mary anointing the feet of Jesus with expensive perfumes. Jesus knows that his entry into Jerusalem means that his death is close, and that perfumes are used to prepare bodies for burial. A: Matthew 21:1–11; B: Mark 11:1–10; C: Luke 19:28–40

Passion Sunday, or Palm Sunday

This drama recalls the Gospel readings that are used in connection with Jesus' triumphal entry into Jerusalem. Those readings are used for the procession that begins the celebration of Passion Sunday, or Palm Sunday. If you would like a drama that focuses on Jesus' Passion, consider the one for Good Friday.

Gospel Readings and Themes

Cycle A. Matthew 21:1–11. Daughter of Zion, your king comes to you.
Cycle B. Mark 11:1–10. Hosanna! Blessed is he who comes in the name of the Lord.
Cycle C. Luke 19:28–40. The very stones would cry out!

Preparation for the Drama
(See resource intro–A, "Leader's Tasks.")

Roles

Catechist, who coordinates the drama
Lector, who leads the opening prayer and proclaims the sacred Scriptures
Gospel players, who enflesh the roles in the scriptural drama

- John
- James
- Peter
- Judas
- Jesus
- Andrew
- Multitude
- Woman 1
- Woman 2
- Man 1

- Man 2
- Sadducee 1
- Sadducee 2
- Pharisee in the Crowd
- Councilman 1
- Joseph of Arimathea
- Councilman 2
- High Priest Annas
- High Priest Caiaphas

Costume Trunk Items

A lectionary or Bible, robes, headdresses, veils, cloaks, and palms

Presentation of the Drama
(See resource intro–A, "Leader's Tasks.")

Script for the Background Reading

Catechist. This Sunday, church members all over the world will take palms into their hands and proclaim "Hosanna!" and re-enact the Passion story during the liturgy. As early as the third century after Jesus' Resurrection, the church celebrated Palm Sunday in this way.

Our scene today begins on the first Palm Sunday. The time of Passover is at hand. Passover is an invitation from God to remember eternally that humanity is created free. It is the festival of salvation that perpetually memorializes the Exodus, the sacred journey in which Moses led the Israelites out of bondage in Egypt.

People all over Jerusalem are rushing to prepare their homes and businesses for the feast. The city and the surrounding area are swarming with pilgrims. Jewish Law requires that all men living within twenty miles of the city must come to Jerusalem to honor the Passover. More than two and a half million pilgrims are traveling from all over the empire to celebrate the feast in the holy city. A quarter of a million lambs will be butchered for the seder that memorializes forever that the Lord God of Israel hears the people's cry and leads humanity always to freedom.

Jerusalem has not known freedom for forty years. Rome controls the city, its people, and the Temple. Passover is both a political and a religious feast. And the air is thick with talk of rebellion. The news that Jesus is on his way to Jerusalem is making this year extremely tense. A multitude of people are rushing to follow Jesus the miracle worker and healer into the city. Hope and the promise of freedom are in the air. The authorities are not happy about it at all.

Script for the Gospel Reading

[The lector leads everyone in prayer while holding up a lectionary or Bible for all to see.]

Lector. Lord Jesus, when problems in our world leave us confused and without hope, let us remember that you go before us in all things. You and your gospel of peace and justice can change the world. With you, we pray to your Father, God, that the divine will for compassion will take root in every heart.

[The lector proclaims the Gospel reading for the current cycle from the lectionary or Bible. Upon finishing, the lector leads the group in response to the Gospel, again holding up the lectionary or Bible for all to see.]

Lector. The Gospel of our Lord Jesus Christ.

Group. Thanks be to God.

Script for the Gospel Drama

[The catechist announces to the group the title of the Gospel scene to be dramatized.]

Catechist. "Blessed Is He Who Comes in the Name of the Lord"

[The catechist describes the Gospel scene to the group.]

Catechist. As the excitement and tension of the approaching Passover mount in the streets of Jerusalem, Jesus chooses his moment to enter the ancient city of David as the Messiah. Like prophets before him, he uses a staged religious and historical drama to announce that the time is at hand.

When Jesus takes to the back of a colt or donkey, the population recognizes his call to freedom. The liberator Judas Maccabee staged a similar demonstration two centuries before, as he defeated the Syrian warlords who then controlled Jerusalem.

If Jesus had ridden a large horse, that action would have spoken of war. Choosing to ride a humbler animal identifies Jesus' mission as a peacemaker. But it seems that the multitude misunderstands the meaning of Jesus' action. They take palms and cry "Hosanna!"—an action that is part of a well-known ancient ritual for welcoming a conquering warlord. The authorities surely think that Jesus is igniting a flame of violence.

Therefore, to the followers of Jesus, the first Palm Sunday signals the beginning of the reign of Jesus, the Christ, the King of the Jews. An event that is not warmly accepted by either Jewish authorities or Roman rulers in Jerusalem.

John. Lord, we're near Jerusalem.

James. Do we have to go to Jerusalem this time of year, Lord? Let's go back to Caesarea Philippi or back to Galilee or even into the hill country of Judea. Let's take the road back to Jericho. Do we really have to go into Jerusalem? There are people everywhere—it might be dangerous.

John. We always go up to Jerusalem for the great feasts.

Peter. We will be okay. Everywhere the mobs are talking about Lazarus, whom Jesus raised from the dead. It's like a carnival around here. We can stay with Joseph of Arimathea when we get to the city. Joseph will keep us safe.

Judas. Why do you fools trust that man? He's a member of the Sanhedrin. The council is very concerned with Jesus.

Jesus. The time is at hand. We must travel to Jerusalem. I long to gather the people of Jerusalem as a hen gathers her chicks under her wings, but they have been unwilling. If they will not hear, they will be compelled to see.

John. Why is Jesus quoting the Book of Kings?

Judas. He's always quoting something.

Andrew. We're almost to Bethany, near the Mount of Olives. We're getting really close to Jerusalem.

John. Great! I'm hungry. Anybody in the mood for some figs and dates? There are lodgings in Bethany. We can have dinner.

Judas. John, you're such a child! Don't you get it? We're in danger! Why do we have this twelve-year-old boy with us?

Jesus. Go into the village. There you'll find a tethered donkey with her colt. Loose them, and bring them to me. If anyone says anything to you, say, "The Master needs them." They'll give them to you.

Peter. So it is fulfilled . . .

James. What are you talking about, Peter?

Peter. Shout for joy, Daughter of Zion, Israel, shout aloud.

Andrew.

> Look, your king is coming to you,
> humble, and mounted on a donkey,
> and on a colt, the foal of a donkey.

Catechist. Jesus is the rightful King of the Jews, Messiah of the house of David. His reign is the reign of love, the reign of the human heart. He is a king who will come humbly riding on a simple donkey, not in a chariot, not on a horse of war. His performance will be a sign of peace. His strength will be the power of love. But not everyone will understand or embrace his mission.

Judas. Great! Peter, can't you see how crazy this is? Jesus thinks he's the fulfillment of the prophecies of Zechariah, who five hundred years ago described a Messiah entering Jerusalem on the foal of a donkey. Jesus thinks he's like Judas Maccabee defeating the tyrant Antiochus. This is madness. We have no army. Rome will destroy us. Is he really going to do this?! Jesus thinks he's Messiah. Do something!

Peter. You're right, Judas. Jesus thinks he's Messiah. The problem *is,* you don't.

Judas. The tension in the air is thick, with Roman soldiers parading their sharp, short swords.

Peter. You can do what you want; I'm going into the village of Bethany to get the donkey and her foal that Jesus has arranged to be waiting for him.

Andrew. Jesus has many friends in Bethany. It won't be difficult to borrow a donkey and colt.

Judas. Really? So what are we supposed to do? Go into the town and say: "Hi, I'm a follower of Jesus. I need your donkeys so we can *stage a revolution.*" We have no soldiers, no swords, no weapons of any kind. Just a holy man riding on a jackass. Peter, have you lost your mind? No one will give you their animals to lead a parade that will end in slaughter. This is crazy. Be rational.

Peter. Jesus has arranged for the animals. When their owners hear the passwords "the Master needs them," they will know that the time is at hand.

Andrew. Are you with him or against him, Judas?

Catechist. When the disciples reach the village, the donkey and colt are ready as Jesus said, and the disciples spread their cloaks on the animals' backs to prepare them for the ride into the city of Jerusalem. As Jesus mounts the donkey, a great crowd begins to gather. They understand the meaning within Jesus' action. Recognizing him as Messiah, the multitude shouts a great "Hosanna!" the war cry of freedom, of salvation.

Multitude. *[Waving palms]* Hosanna to the Son of David! Blessed is he who comes in the name of the Lord. Hosanna in the highest!

Catechist. One by one, the people spread their cloaks on the road as he passes. Recognizing him as a prophet of wisdom, they run to cut down palm branches and cover the streets with them.

Multitude. Hosanna to the Son of David! Blessed is he who comes in the name of the Lord. Hosanna in the highest!

Woman 1. The whole city has gone wild. Who is this man who raised Lazarus from the dead? I wonder if he can bring back Moses.

Woman 2. He's the prophet Jesus. He comes from Nazareth in Galilee. Hallelujah! Hallelujah, Jesus!

Man 1. Galilee! Nothing good ever came out of Galilee! Look, they're acting like this Galilean is some kind of conqueror. The authorities will go into despair. This Jesus is really popular. How come I don't know about him?

Woman 2. 'Cause you're too busy sightseeing. Rumor has it, he can heal the blind, the deaf, the lame, the brokenhearted. And he's really respectful to women. He's known for loving his mother.

Multitude. Hosanna! Blessed is he who comes in the name of the Lord! Hallelujah! Praise God!

Man 2. This looks like trouble. *[To woman 1]* Woman, we're going home.

Multitude. Hosanna to the Son of David! Blessed is he who comes in the name of the Lord. Hosanna in the highest!

Woman 1. No, Husband, look. He enters the city on a donkey, like Zechariah.

Woman 2. Daughter of Jerusalem, your king comes to you, gentle, and riding upon an ass. He has chosen a foal that has never been ridden before. This is a ceremony with a sacred purpose.

Multitude. Hosanna to the Son of David! Blessed is he who comes in the name of the Lord. Hosanna in the highest!

Woman 1. The Law speaks of a red heifer used for cleansing. Jesus is cleansing the city, riding a beast upon which a yoke has never come.

Woman 2. He is presenting himself like the ark of the Covenant, which was lost after Babylon. Like when Jehu was proclaimed king, the people spread their cloaks in front of him. They are calling Jesus *King.*

Man 1. Is this Jesus promising a conquest? a rebellion? Lord, we have waited so long. It's a conqueror's welcome the people shout: "Blessed is he who comes in the name of the Lord."

Man 2. "He who comes!" Everyone knows that "he who comes" is a description of the Messiah. The Messiah is the *One who is coming.* The people call Jesus *Messiah, Savior!*

Multitude. Hosanna to the Son of David! Blessed is he who comes in the name of the Lord. Hosanna in the highest!

Man 1. Do you remember what the elders teach? After Simon Maccabee entered Jerusalem following his victory over Antiochus, the people waved palms and cried: "Messiah! *Hosanna!*"

Multitude. Save us! *Hosanna!* Free us from bondage, liberate us, oh, Lord. Lead your mighty cherubim to defend your people! *Hosanna* in the highest! Save us now!

Woman 2. Jesus is welcomed as *Deliverer, Savior, and King!*

Catechist. The Psalms record the ancient cry "Save us, Lord." They shout *"Hosanna!"* the ancient war cry of freedom. But not everyone welcomes Messiah's entry into Jerusalem. The Romans see it as a threat to their power. The Jewish Council of priests see it as the beginning of a revolution.

[In the Temple council]

Sadducee 1. This meeting of the Sanhedrin is in order. We have to stop this rebellion. We have to stop Jesus. He's going to cause a riot! Does this man have a follower who is rational, who can see how dangerous this is? The Romans aren't going to like this at all.

Sadducee 2. Why should the Romans like this display of rebellion? They've worked hard. They worked with us Sadducees to control the people. You know what this Jesus is saying with his prophetic demonstration. He's dramatically alluding to our control. He's boldly comparing us to Antiochus and his blasphemies in the Temple. He's challenging what we do in the Temple as well. Jesus is trouble. Jesus must be eliminated.

Sadducee 1. That can't be. You're overreacting. We perform the rites. We are Law abiding. Antiochus scandalously offered swine's flesh on the altar, sacrificed to the Olympian Zeus, and turned the Temple chambers into public brothels. We have hardly done that. Jesus is just a holy man, like so many before him entering Jerusalem at Passover. He's really no problem.

Sadducee 2. You naive *do-gooder.* Get your head out of the sand. This Jesus took a whip to the Temple's animal stalls. This is just another of his *cleansing* demonstrations, you fool. Remember the writing in which the Maccabees waved branches of palms and sang psalms to celebrate the cleansing of the Temple. Jesus is staging a *prophetic condemnation* of our arrangement with Rome.

Sadducee 1. You're right. That is almost exactly what Jesus and his followers are doing. He's cleansing the city. Oh, the nerve of this Galilean. This is quite deliberate. He's intentionally cleansing God's house, just like Judas Maccabee did a hundred and fifty years ago. This is bad.

Sadducee 2. We're helpless to stop this Jesus. The whole world has gone off after him!

Sadducee 1. He's an outlaw. I'm determined to have him arrested.

Multitude. Blessed is the King who comes in the name of the Lord! Peace in heaven and glory in the highest.

[Among the disciples, who have followed Jesus in the crowd]

Peter. The prophet Malachi said that the Lord would come to his Temple? Jesus *went* to the Temple.

Andrew. The psalms sang of his coming: "Behold, O Lord, and raise up unto them their king."

Peter. The Son of David, who would purge Jerusalem from nations.

James. Ezekiel saw the terrible judgment of God beginning at the Sanctuary.

John. Peter, the people are calling Jesus *the Anointed of God!*

James. The whole world has gone off after him!

Judas. Look, fools for Christ, this is dangerous. King of the Jews! Peter, we have got to stop him. He's gone mad. This is suicide. If we stay with him, we're dead. Who does he think he is?

Peter. He thinks he's the Son of God, the Promised One. *Hosanna!* Blessed is the One who will lead us to freedom.

Andrew. The people praise him as the *One* who will save them from bondage.

John. I believe him.

Peter. So do they.

Judas. Today the mob cries "Hosanna!" They think he will free them from Rome. What will they think when the soldiers get here? What will happen if we follow him?

Peter. What will happen to the world if we don't?

Pharisee in the Crowd. Teacher, rebuke your disciples. Make them stop. This is going to cause trouble with the authorities.

Jesus. If the people are silenced, *the very stones will cry out.*

Catechist. Not everyone who meets Jesus can hear the Good News. For some, his teachings are unbearable. They see that the Gospel of Christ requires changing ways of thinking and acting that have been revered and strictly enforced for generations. How can Jesus expect them to turn their whole world upside down? How can love require tolerance and justice for people toward whom the ancient way teaches segregation and prejudice? For some in authority, the answer becomes clear—destroy Jesus, and silence his disturbing teachings. These people think that if they execute Jesus as a blasphemous subversive, the traitor will be forgotten.

The council members of the Sanhedrin and the high priests are such people. They feel that their power is challenged by Jesus and they want him eliminated. Joseph of Arimathea is a member of the Sanhedrin as well as a secret follower of Christ. It breaks his heart to hear of the plot to stop the mission of Jesus. He does what he can to halt the wave of hatred. But in the end, he will only be able to offer Jesus a tomb he has made for himself.

[Within the Sanhedrin]

Councilman 1. The priests are against him.

Joseph of Arimathea. The zealots call him a pacifist. He won't challenge Rome. He causes no problem.

Councilman 2. He ignores the fact that we're in bondage.

Councilman 1. I'm terrified that Pilate is going to avenge these maniacs following him around, talking about a new kingdom and a new king.

Joseph. He's no danger.

Councilman 2. He's merely deluded.

Joseph. Have you heard him? He says to forgive your enemies, turn the other cheek. He teaches the law of compassion.

Councilman 1. The man's a fool. *[Laughing]*

Councilman 2. Give unto Caesar what is Caesar's, and unto God what is God's. Very good politics. Jesus' Kingdom is at hand?

Joseph. His Kingdom is not of this world.

Councilman 1. Smart guy . . .

Councilman 2. He will be forgotten.

High Priest Annas. We can't stop him now. Look—the whole world is running after him.

Joseph. He's not hurting anybody.

Councilman 2. Just another deluded religious fanatic.

Joseph. Leave him alone.

Annas. You don't seem to have grasped the situation at all. You fail to see that it's better for one man to die for the people than for the whole nation to be destroyed.

High Priest Caiaphas. This Jesus must die for the nation, for the unity of the scattered children of God, or Rome will destroy us.

Annas. Jesus must die.

Caiaphas. Jesus must die.

Sanhedrin in union, except for Joseph. Jesus must die.

Catechist. Jesus had devoted his last three years on earth to an important mission—proclaiming the good news of salvation to all of humanity. Jesus was a conqueror who defeated evil with love. He was a warrior against prejudice and injustice. Jesus, the divine Messiah incarnate, offered himself as the love of God—*hesed,* unconditional, unchanging, and eternal—to everyone who would listen. Jesus was the king, prophet, and priest of the Reign of God. The healings Jesus performed and his teachings, parables, mercy, and compassion all pointed to a new law of love that is purer and higher than other laws, a way of life that brings freedom and hope.

This Jesus was not the kind of conqueror or military leader the multitude had expected. A week after his triumphal entry into Jerusalem, another mob demanded that the Roman governor of Judea set free the imprisoned warrior zealot Barabbas and send the Prince of

Peace to Calvary. Governor Pontius Pilate did as the mob desired and condemned Jesus to be crucified.

We have come to the place in our Lenten journey where our catechumens choose to follow Christ as members of the Catholic family of believers and the baptized recommit their loyalty to our Lord and the Christian community. Who are we in today's story? Are we part of the fickle multitude who this week cry "Hosanna" and next week cry, "Crucify him"? Are we Peter, loyal but afraid of what it means to follow Jesus? Or are we Judas, more concerned with the world than with the Glory in our midst? As we contemplate the last act in the drama of the life of Jesus, we are asked to go inside ourselves and to examine our spirit. To ask ourselves if our spirit is in union with the Spirit of Christ.

Follow-up After the Drama
(See resource intro–A, "Leader's Tasks.")

Reflection Questions

- What does Jesus' triumphal entry into Jerusalem tell us about how he understood his mission?
- How are we called to show ourselves publicly as followers of Christ in our world?
- How does this story speak to the kind of king Jesus is?
- How does this story speak to the kind of kingdom Jesus wants his church to become?
- How does this story speak to the kind of followers Jesus desires us to become?

Improv
(See resource intro–A, "Leader's Tasks.")

Closure
(See resource intro–A, "Leader's Tasks.")

Illustration by Vicki Shuck

Holy Thursday Icon

By washing the disciples' feet and later sharing himself in food and drink, Jesus shows us how to live God's love. All cycles: John 13:1–5

Holy Thursday

Gospel Reading and Theme

All cycles. John 13:1–5. Jesus washes the feet of the disciples.

Preparation for the Drama

(See resource intro–A, "Leader's Tasks.")

Roles

Catechist, who coordinates the drama
Lector, who leads the opening prayer and proclaims the sacred Scriptures
Gospel players, who enflesh the roles in the scriptural drama

- Peter
- James the Son of Zebedee
- John
- Messenger
- Master of the Household
- priests in the Temple (mimed roles)
- Jesus
- Judas
- Thomas
- Andrew
- Matthew
- Bartholomew
- Thaddeus (whom the tradition calls Jude)
- Philip
- James the Son of Alphaeus
- Simon the Zealot

Costume Trunk Items

A lectionary or Bible, robes, headdresses, a water jar, a candle and matches, a stuffed lamb, a gold or silver bowl, a plate of cooked lamb (or other meat; optional), pita (unleavened) bread, bitter herbs (optional), *haroseth* (optional), sticks of cinnamon (optional), a bowl of saltwater (optional), cups of juice (for wine; optional), cushions (to represent couches in the upper room), a towel, a pitcher of water and a basin (for foot washing), a chalice of juice (for wine), and a second basin of water (for hand washing)

🎭 Presentation of the Drama
(See resource intro–A, "Leader's Tasks.")

Script for the Background Reading

Catechist. All of Jerusalem prepared for the festival of unleavened bread, or Passover. Gathered with the disciples in an upper room, Jesus said the prayers of the Jewish seder, blessed the unleavened bread, broke it, and gave thanks. Then he commissioned his followers to celebrate this feast perpetually, in sacred memory of him. It was to be Jesus' Last Supper.

Two thousand years have gone by since that Passover night, and we, his disciples, still break bread and offer eucharistic thanksgiving to honor and bond ourselves to our Lord. The words "Do this in memory of me" are an invitation to enter into the sacramental reality in which the body, mind, soul, and divinity of Christ are truly present in the consecrated bread and wine offered at the Mass. We hold this gift from Jesus as the foundation and source of our faith.

Celebrating the eucharistic liturgy is an active encounter with Jesus in our midst. Christ takes flesh in the bread and wine of our sacrifice. His body and blood are offered to us as food to nourish and prepare us for the Christian life. When we accept them, we choose as our most precious value our relationships with Jesus and with one another as church.

Script for the Gospel Reading

[The lector leads everyone in prayer while holding up a lectionary or Bible for all to see.]

Lector. Jesus, you are the Bread of Life, the Lamb of God who takes away the sins of the world. Thank you for calling us into your love. We pray to hunger for communion with you in the Blessed Sacrament of the Eucharist. We offer ourselves as a channel of your peace, as an instrument for justice. Empower us all with the grace of our baptism, to fully embrace your call to come, follow you. We pray for vocations—priestly, religious, and lay—in service of your Gospel. May we all commit our lives to your gospel of peace and love.

[The lector proclaims the Gospel reading from the lectionary or Bible. Upon finishing, the lector leads the group in response to the Gospel, again holding up the lectionary or Bible for all to see.]

Lector. The Gospel of our Lord Jesus Christ.

Group. Thanks be to God.

Script for the Gospel Drama

[The catechist announces to the group the title of the Gospel scene to be dramatized.]

Catechist. "Lamb of God, Bread of Life"

[The catechist describes the Gospel scene to the group.]

Catechist. The Eucharist we celebrate enfleshes the Passion of Jesus in our midst. We offer the Mass in gratitude, as a sign that Christ is present in all we say and do. As we say "Amen," we commit ourselves to the belief that the gift of God's love and the salvation offered through this sacrament are the absolute reality of Christ our Lord, body and soul.

Those who are baptized in Christ proclaim that salvation is at hand. Christ, Emmanuel, is with us. Through the love of Jesus, we are liberated from the slavery of our sins. We are forgiven and made new. We are in communion with Christ. Sacramentally, this is same reality that Jesus offered to his disciples on the night before he suffered. On this Holy Thursday night, as we reverently prepare to honor our Lord through the liturgy of the Eucharist, we are in communion with our ancestors of faith, those disciples who prepared for Jesus' Last Supper on the night before he suffered.

Peter. This is what he told us to do.

James the Son of Zebedee. How are we to know the place?

John. Jesus said he prepared a place.

Peter. Jesus said that we would see a man carrying a water jar.

James the Son of Zebedee. Men don't carry water jars. That's women's work.

Peter. Well, a man carrying a water jar is the sign Jesus wants. We are to approach him. He will lead us to the room where we will have the seder together with our Lord.

James the Son of Zebedee. There he is, water jar and all.

Peter. Sir, the Teacher asks for a guest room where he may eat the Passover with his disciples.

Messenger. We have prepared an upper room. It is a large room, furnished and ready. Come and you can prepare for the Passover of the Lord. The master of the house is expecting you.

Catechist. Peter, James, and John approach the house that has been prepared for the feast by an unknown disciple. They enter from an outside stairway that leads up the side of the building. The disciples walk through the main room of the house into the upper room and begin the preparations according to sacred Jewish custom.

Master of the Household. I am honored to offer my home for Jesus. Shall we begin? Here is the candle for the purification ritual.

Peter. Thank you. Let us sanctify this home, give thanks to our God, and prepare for the seder. Blessed art thou, Lord, our God, King of the Universe. You have sanctified us by your law and commanded us to remove the leaven from our homes.

Catechist. In all observant Jewish households, preparations for the seder begin with a ceremonial search for leaven, which is fermented dough. This symbol of corruption must be banished from the house in honor of the first Passover, during which the Israelites ate unleavened bread. So the disciples take a lighted candle and ceremonially search the house for leaven.

Master of the Household. All the leaven that is in my possession, that which I have seen and that which I have not seen, is gone, accounted for as the dust of the earth.

Catechist. The preparations continue with the sacrifice of a lamb. *[A disciple and a number of priests reverently mime this ritual as the catechist describes it.]* One of the disciples approaches the priests in the Temple with a lamb of sacrifice. The lamb is quickly and painlessly killed, and the blood is collected in a gold or silver bowl. The bowl of blood is passed from priest to priest, and the last priest offers it upon the altar. The lamb is then butchered. The entrails and the fat are left in the Temple as a sacrifice. The meat is returned to the disciple, who takes it back to the house to be ceremoniously roasted over an open fire of pomegranate wood.

[The disciple returns to the upper room.]

John. Peter, the women have prepared the lamb. The feast is almost ready.

[The disciples may bring each item for the feast to the table as they discuss it in the following speeches:]

Peter. With this lamb we remember that the Lord protected the houses of the Israelites from the plague of death. The angel of death passed over the houses marked with the blood of the lamb. We offer to the master of this house the skin of the lamb that was prepared for our feast, as payment for his generosity.

Master of the House. I am honored.

James the Son of Zebedee. The women have prepared the unleavened bread. This is the night we remember our salvation from the bondage of Egypt.

Peter. Here are the bitter herbs—horseradish, chicory, endive, lettuce, and horehound—used to help us remember the bitterness of slavery.

James the Son of Zebedee. Here is the *haroseth*—the paste of apples, dates, pomegranates, and nuts—to honor the memory of the clay from which our ancestors were forced to make bricks in Egypt.

John. And sticks of cinnamon to remind us of the straw that was mixed with the clay.

Peter. We use this bowl of saltwater to remember the tears our ancestors shed and the sea through which the Israelites passed to freedom.

John. And everyone has four cups of wine?

Peter. The wine of blessing reminds us of the four promises the Lord made to our ancestors. We have celebrated this Passover since the time of Moses. Our fathers and mothers before us and those who come in the future will remember for all time that *this night is different from every other night.*

[Jesus and the rest of the twelve Apostles enter the upper room.]

Peter. James, John, look: Jesus has arrived.

Catechist. It is time to begin the feast. Jesus gathers his disciples around a low, square table, inviting them to recline on couches.

John. Lord, we have been so worried about you. All this talk in the streets! Why do so many people mistrust and hate you when we all love you so much? But all that matters is that you're here for the Passover supper at last. Will you sit here next to me?

Jesus. I would love to sit beside you, John. I have longed to eat this Passover supper with you.

James the Son of Zebedee. No, let me sit next to you, Lord. John, you're always sitting next to Jesus. Give someone else a chance. Just because you're the youngest—

Peter. I am the rock. The leader. I will sit next to Jesus.

Jesus. The Father has given all things into my hands. I have come from God and I am going to God. Those who offer their lives in service to others will receive the highest place of honor in my Kingdom.

Catechist. *[Jesus and the disciples act out the following foot-washing ceremony as the catechist speaks:]* Jesus gets up from the table, takes off his outer robe, and ties a towel around himself. Then he pours water into a basin and begins to wash the disciples' feet and to wipe them with his towel.

Peter. Lord, are you going to wash my feet?

Jesus. I know that my washing the disciples' feet is confusing to you, Peter. But later you will understand.

Peter. You will never wash my feet.

Jesus. Unless I wash you, you have no share with me.

Peter. Lord, then wash not only my feet, but my hands and my head as well.

Jesus. Those who have bathed do not need to wash, except for the feet. You are clean. But one among us is not clean.

Catechist. Jesus is speaking to Judas. The Lord knows Judas plans to betray him.

After Jesus has washed the feet of the disciples, he puts on his robe and returns to the table.

Jesus. Do you know what my washing your feet means?

John. You have made us clean, Lord?

Jesus. You call me Teacher and Lord—and you are right, for that is what I am. So if I—your Lord and Teacher—have washed your feet, you must wash one another's feet. Let this be an example to you. Do to one another as I have done to you.

Judas. That is below our station. Washing feet is the work of slaves. I want no part of it!

Jesus. Very truly, I tell you, servants are not greater than their master, nor are messengers greater than the one who sent them. God creates all of us as equals. I ask you to be servants in my Kingdom. Blessed are you who serve humanity for the Reign of God. Peter, let us begin the seder prayers.

Peter. Blessed be our Lord, our God, Creator of the Universe; you bring goodness from the earth.

John. What makes this night different from all other nights?

Peter. Tender lamb, unleavened bread, wine and bitter herbs, prayers and song—it is a celebration of a freed people.

James the Son of Zebedee. This is the night we light the candles.

Thomas. We look into one another's eyes and toast the ancestors, prophets—

Judas. —and kings.

All the Apostles. We see . . . the salvation . . . of our God.

Peter. This night we eat meat with our staff in our hand, our sandals on our feet, and a belt around our waist.

Thomas. We eat hastily, a meal in flight, for it is Passover.

Andrew. For God said, "When the angel of death sees the blood of the lamb, it will pass over you—

Matthew. —and you will escape the destroying plague.

Bartholomew. You will be free."

Thaddeus. This is a day of remembrance, this is the day of Passover.

Philip. For the angel of death passed over the houses of the Israelites.

Thomas. And the plague of death struck the land of Egypt.

James the Son of Alphaeus. The Lord heard our people's cry and they were freed from slavery.

All the Apostles. We . . . were . . . *saved!*

Simon the Zealot. For all generations of all time, we are to declare this occasion a day of festival, forever.

Thomas. Sing to the Lord, for the Lord has triumphed gloriously.

Philip. The horse and rider the Lord has thrown into the sea.

James the Son of Alphaeus. For the Lord has brought us out of the land of Egypt—

Thaddeus. —and redeemed us from the house of bondage.

Andrew. The Lord has brought us to the Promised Land—

Matthew. —a land flowing with milk and honey.

Peter. Praise, O servants of the Lord. Blessed be the name of the Lord from this time on and forevermore.

Jesus. *[Holding up a chalice of wine]* This is the cup of Haggadah, the proclaiming. Let us purify our hands.

[Jesus and the Apostles wash their hands in a fresh basin of water.]

Jesus. *[Holding up a piece of pita bread]* Blessed are you, O God. You
have sanctified us with the Law and commanded us to eat this bread.
I have desired, with all my heart, to eat this Passover with you before
I suffer. I will not eat again until my suffering is finished, until I do so in
the Kingdom of God. Blessed are you, Father in heaven, who gives us
this day our daily bread.

I break this bread in memory of our affliction in Egypt when our
ancestors were slaves. Let the hungry come and eat. Let the poor come
and keep this Passover with us.

Catechist. Rabbi Jesus has celebrated the Passover as it is always celebrated. But this night is different from all other nights. On this Passover,
Jesus will offer himself as the Lamb of God. And on this night, now, he
offers his presence in bread and wine so that his disciples will remember that sacrifice. He takes the bread, gives thanks, blesses and breaks
the bread, and gives it to the disciples, saying:

Jesus. I am the Lamb of God, who takes away the sins of the world. Blessed
are you who come to this table. Take and eat . . . all of you. This is
my body, to be given up for you. Do this in memory of me.

All the Apostles. Lamb of God, who takes away the sins of the world, have
mercy on us.

Catechist. For the Catholic Christian, the liturgy of the Eucharist is the
sacrament of the presence of God. It is the icon that offers an encounter of love with the mind, body, blood, soul, and divinity of Jesus.
Repeating the words Jesus spoke in his Eucharist Passover, on the
night before he suffered, forms the family of the New Covenant. In
every Mass, in every country, for all time, we, his followers, remember
our Lord Jesus. In all we say and do, we remember him as the incarnate Son of the Holy One, who eternally and continually gives himself
to us as the sacrament of the Eucharist for the salvation of our souls.

Catechist. Jesus takes the cup of the Kiddush, the cup of sanctification,
and, blessing it, continues the seder.

Jesus. *[Holding up the chalice]* I offer this cup in thanksgiving. Blessed
are you, O Lord, our God, Creator of the Universe, who has created the
fruit of the vine.

Peter. Let us sing the great Hallelujah. O give thanks to the Lord, for the
Lord is good.

All the Apostles. The Lord's mercy and steadfast love endure forever.

Thomas. O give thanks to the God of heaven.

All the Apostles. The Lord's mercy and steadfast love endure forever.

Jesus. This is the cup of my blood, of the new and everlasting covenant.
It will be shed for you . . . so that sins will be forgiven. Do this in
memory of me. I will never again drink of this fruit of the vine until that
day when I drink it new with you in my Father's Kingdom.

Matthew. What does it all mean, Lord? We want you with us. We couldn't
go on without you. We need you. Now more than ever.

Jesus. Trust me. Tonight we celebrate the paschal feast together as a sign of our unity.

I hold this bread in my hands, I give thanks for it, bless it, break it . . . and I share it with all of you. This is my body.

This cup is the New Covenant made at the price of my blood, which is shed for you.

One of you will betray me, one of you at this table. One of you will betray me this night. My friend who has dipped his hand into the bowl with me will betray me. It is written of the betrayer: "Woe to that one by whom the Son of Man is betrayed! It would have been better for him that he had not ever been born."

All the Apostles. Not I, Lord! I will not betray you. Not I! Not I! . . . Who?

Jesus. As it is written in the Psalms:

> Even my bosom friend in whom I trusted,
> who ate of my bread, has lifted the heel against me.
> But you, O Lord, be gracious to me,
> and raise me up.
>
> . . . .
>
> Blessed be the Lord, the God of Israel,
> from everlasting to everlasting.

Peter. No, Lord, this is impossible! Who is it? I'll break his neck.

James the Son of Zebedee. Lord, we love you, we would never betray you.

Judas. Surely not I, Rabbi?

Peter. What is he saying? One of us, Lord, your betrayer? Not I, Lord, not I.

John. Lord, that can't be. What does he mean?

James the Son of Alphaeus. It can't be one of us Lord. Not I, Lord, not I.

Jesus. I want you never to betray one another, but to love one another. Let the greater among you be as the servant. I am in your midst tonight as the one who serves you. Follow my example. I have prayed for you that your faith may never fail, and you must each strengthen one another.

Peter. Though all become deserters because of you, I will never desert you.

Jesus. Peter, before the cock crows, you will deny me three times.

Peter. Never!

Catechist. The Apostle Judas leaves the party and steals into the night to betray the Lord. The chief priests pay him thirty pieces of silver to lead them to Jesus. The chief priests and scribes plot to have Jesus arrested and brought to the Roman governor Pilate. They accuse Jesus of seditious agitation; leading his followers to refuse payment of a tribute to Caesar; claiming the title of king; and blasphemy, daring to call himself the Son of God.

All over the world on Holy Thursday, the universal community of Christ gathers to celebrate that Passover feast when our Lord instituted the sacrament of the Eucharist, our communion with him. Gathered by the Messiah, we are called to use sign, sacrament, and symbol to keep God's saving acts present across the span of history. That long-ago night celebrated in memoriam proclaims hope in the face of all oppression, perpetually recalling that deliverance and justice were and are God's will, even before death on a cross. Together we pray, "Dying you destroyed our death, / rising you restored our life."

Follow-up After the Drama
(See resource intro–A, "Leader's Tasks.")

Reflection Questions

- How do you think those first disciples felt on that first Holy Thursday night when Jesus invited them to share the sacrament of his love?
- How do you think they felt when he was betrayed and arrested?
- What is the most precious human love you have ever known? How do you feel being that loved? Some people believe that they have never known love. How would that feel?
- How old were you when you celebrated your first Eucharist? What do you remember about the first time you received the sacrament?
- What is your experience of the Eucharist now? How do you prepare yourself for encountering Jesus in the most holy sacrament of the altar?
- When you think that Jesus gave *his very self* to nourish our souls, how does that most deep love make you feel?
- How would you describe the experience of encountering Jesus the Christ in the sacrament of the Eucharist to a person who has never known Christ?

Improv
(See resource intro–A, "Leader's Tasks.")

Closure
(See resource intro–A, "Leader's Tasks.")

Good Friday Icon

The time has come for Jesus to put his own life on the line for all that he has taught about God. The whole truth of Jesus' life rests on his willingness to give himself to death. Passion Sunday, or Palm Sunday, A: Matthew 26:14–27,66; B: Mark 14:1–47; C: Luke 22:14–56. Good Friday, all cycles: John, chapters 18–19.

Good Friday

The Passion of Christ, though deeply sorrowful, shines for all time as the greatest gift of love ever offered to humanity. Jesus, who is God, took human flesh and dwelled among us so that his earthly mission could culminate in this one perfect sacrifice of love. Jesus conquered death so that, blessedly, our own lives and the lives of those we love are welcomed into eternal life. We honor his Passion and death in the following dramas, based on the fourteen stations of the cross and the sorrowful mysteries of the rosary. The stations help us reflect on the events of Good Friday, and they also can be used with the accounts of the Passion in the synoptic Gospels, which are read on Passion Sunday, or Palm Sunday.

Gospel Readings and Themes

Passion Sunday, or Palm Sunday
Cycle A. Matthew 26:14–27,66. The Passion of Jesus Christ.
Cycle B. Mark 14:1–47. The Passion of Jesus Christ.
Cycle C. Luke 22:14–56. The Passion of Jesus Christ.

Good Friday
All cycles. John, chapters 18–19. Arrest, judgment, death, and burial.

Preparation for the Drama
(See resource intro–A, "Leader's Tasks.")

Roles

A separate cast of characters is announced for each station. The following roles appear in all fourteen stations:
Catechist, who coordinates the drama
Lector, who leads the opening and closing prayers and proclaims the sacred
    Scriptures
Gospel players, who enflesh the roles in the scriptural drama
- Multitude, comprising the audience, or all in the room
- Chorus, comprising the catechist, the lector, and the Gospel players

Costume Trunk Items

A lectionary or Bible, robes, headdresses, veils, a scarlet cloak, a reed representing a scepter, a crown of thorns, Roman soldier uniforms and spears, a large wooden cross or a beam of wood representing the cross, a whip, "Veronica's veil," a hammer and nails, a flask or jar of juice (for wine), and a sponge

Presentation of the Drama
(See resource intro–A, "Leader's Tasks.")

Script for the Background Reading

Catechist. Good Friday is the most somber day of the liturgical year. Entering the church, we sense that this quiet day is different from every other day. The red sanctuary lamp, usually lit by a candle round the clock, round the year, is dark, signifying that the tabernacle is empty. No Mass is celebrated. The altar stands completely bare. Holy water fonts are dry. All of creation mourned at the moment of Christ's death, and those liturgical signs speak to that haunting loss.

    The focal point inside Catholic churches on this day—along with a large crucifix—is a series of fourteen paintings or carvings that hang along the walls. These are the stations of the cross, fourteen icons that memorialize incidents during Christ's final day on earth. They take us step-by-step from the moment Pilate condemned Jesus to the hour of sorrow when Christ's loved ones laid him in the tomb.

    In the following fourteen stations, we reflect on the historical Passion of Jesus and link it to our own sufferings, to the agonies of all humanity. Jesus understands our grief, our pain, our anxiety, and our fear. He has known intimately, in his own flesh, in his own emotions, all the human crosses we carry. He made this promise to Mary of Magdala: *"I go before you."* His life assures us that even the heaviest, most agonizing, and most unjust cross—embraced with love—will lead to glory.

Script for the Gospel Reading

[The lector leads everyone in prayer while holding up a lectionary or Bible for all to see.]

Lector. Lord Jesus, the terror you felt at the hands of your enemies must have crushed your human soul. You had friends who would have hidden you. You could have run away. You could have called a million angels to your rescue. Yet for love of me, you embraced the cross. Why do you love each of us so much? What is it about us that you would pay any price—even a torturous death—to keep us with you forever? This mystery humbles me. Lord, pour the love of your Sacred Heart into my heart, so that I can touch and comfort others in your name.

[The lector proclaims the appropriate Gospel reading for the current cycle from the lectionary or Bible. Upon finishing, the lector leads the group in response to the Gospel, again holding up the lectionary or Bible for all to see.]

Lector. The Gospel of our Lord Jesus Christ.

Group. Thanks be to God.

First Station

Roles

Catechist
Lector
Gospel players
- High Priest Caiaphas
- High Priest Annas
- Multitude
- Pontius Pilate
- Jesus (nonspeaking role)
- Chorus
- Henry
- Susan

Script for the Gospel Drama

[The catechist announces to the group the title of the station to be dramatized.]

Catechist. "First Station: Jesus Is Condemned to Death"

[The catechist describes the Gospel scene to the group.]

Catechist. Everything about Jesus' condemnation was wrong. He was innocent, yet he was arrested, falsely accused, and set up for the death sentence. The chief priests, religious elders, and scribes who orchestrated his destruction claimed to be acting out of righteousness. In truth, their moral indignation was a disguise for ego and jealousy.

Jesus was not allowed a trial as understood by Western standards. After Judas betrayed him, Jesus was taken into the custody of the Sanhedrin and was shamed and humiliated. For the high priests to bring Jesus down, first they had to destroy his reputation.

At the house of the high priest Annas, the whole assembly shamed Jesus in view of a courtyard full of onlookers. Peter was in the crowd. As Jesus' eyes met Peter's, Peter wept bitterly—before his human fear of mortality overtook him and he ran to hide. The priests blindfolded the Lord, struck him from behind, and mocked him as a "prophet."

The high priests then spread rumors against Jesus and organized demonstrations against him outside Pilate's palace. The Gospels record that the high priests and the elders convinced the crowds to ask Pilate to release Barabbas, a criminal condemned to die, and to crucify Jesus. They taunted the people on the streets with their fears of Roman brutality, and demanded that the mob direct its loyalty away from Jesus. Like a lynch mob, the people quickly turned their hearts to murder.

[The high priests, Pilate, and Jesus outside Pilate's palace]

High Priest Caiaphas. *[To the crowds]* Pilate has offered to release a prisoner in honor of the Passover. You better ask for Barabbas. Jesus the Nazarene is a troublemaker.

High Priest Annas. Call for Barabbas, or the unrest that Jesus brings will cause the Romans to crucify hundreds, like they did two years ago. People of Israel, you have the power to save Jerusalem. Jesus must die.

Multitude. We want Barabbas. Crucify Jesus! We want Barabbas. We want Barabbas. Crucify Jesus! We want Barabbas. We have no king but Caesar!

Caiaphas. Governor Pilate, the people are yelling in the streets. Give them what they want, or you will have a riot on your hands!

Multitude. Crucify him! Crucify him! Crucify him!

Caiaphas. You're the one in charge. Our faithful religious people under your jurisdiction are counting on you. What is holding you back? Please hurry, so we can get to the Temple before the Sabbath begins.

Pontius Pilate. Your hatred for this Rabbi mystifies me. I see nothing serious in his attitude, nothing to merit a criminal's death. Look at him! He won't even speak on his own behalf. He's no danger to you. He's really quite passive.

Annas. He is a rebel. He incites the people to violence. His followers run screaming through the streets, waving palms and proclaiming "Hosanna!" He will get us into a war. His sins of blasphemy are scandalous.

Pilate. What does this blasphemy you speak of have to do with me? He is a Jew, one of your own. Deal with him in your own religious circle.

Caiaphas. But Governor Pilate, we have no law to put a man to death. Only Rome has the authority to *eliminate* him. Only you can speak the death sentence. We need you—and, frankly, you need us. We are here to warn you.

Annas. This Jesus claims he's a king. If you release him, you are not Caesar's friend, for whoever makes himself a king speaks against Caesar! We have no king but Caesar.

Caiaphas. Worse by far, he acts like he's God. He enthralls your subjects all over Judea. Soon the people will stop listening to us *and* to you. This man is just as dangerous to Rome as he is to our position as authorities in Jerusalem. He threatens *our arrangement,* Lord Pilate.

Annas. Sentence him! Please hurry, Governor Pilate. The Sabbath approaches. This distasteful event must be finished by sundown.

Pilate. Jesus of Nazareth, do you hear all these accusations against you? Why are you so quiet? Defend yourself. Are you to be the Lamb of Sacrifice?

Caiaphas. He cannot speak because he is guilty. We want crucifixion!

Multitude. We want Barabbas. Crucify Jesus! We want Barabbas. We want Barabbas. Crucify Jesus! We want Barabbas. We have no king but Caesar! Crucify him! Crucify him! Crucify him!

Pilate. Who are you, Jesus? I have the power over your life and death. All I have to do is say the word, and it's your last day on earth. Why aren't you afraid of me, Jesus? Why aren't you afraid of Annas, of Caiaphas, who stand here as your judges? Jesus, I hold your life in my hands. This calm surrounding you makes no sense. What is this peace beyond understanding?

Caiaphas. Don't be fooled. His agenda is far from peaceful. He terrorizes our religious elders. No one can sleep at night. Jesus gives nightmares to the righteous.

Pilate. *[To himself]* Is this the man of whom my wife dreamed? The one of whom she warned me? "Have nothing to do with this man Jesus," she said. She was so frightened. She told me not to permit a hand to be laid on him. Agggg! The foolishness of women.

[To the priests] I want this controversy over. Your Messiah is harmless. He is innocent. But if you want him dead, why should I disappoint you? You're the leaders of the people. I will do with him as you desire. I wash my hands of this Jesus. He's yours. Let his blood be upon *you*. Crucify him! I have spoken.

Chorus. By your holy cross, you have redeemed the world.

Catechist. Jesus, the incarnate Son of God, is judged, condemned, and crucified every time any one of us is suffering. Christ's love for us, his longing to be one with us, is so complete that he continues to suffer until the end of the world, through the grief, pain, alienation, fear, and despairs of humanity. As Mother Teresa of Calcutta taught us, all persons in suffering are Jesus in a miserable disguise.

Henry. I'm on death row, for a murder I didn't do. I didn't kill that guy. No witnesses, no alibi. And nobody cares about it. They all just figure that 'cause I was in the right place at the wrong time, I took him out. I didn't do it. I'm innocent. I didn't even know this guy. I was just walking around and tripped on his body, lying there in the alley. Does anyone care? I'm twenty-three years old and I am going to die. This is breaking my mother's heart.

Susan. He raped me. We were on a date. Yes, I'm pregnant. No one believes my side of the story, even my own parents. They threw me out of the house. That's why I'm on the streets. The guy who raped me tells everybody that I asked for it. They all judge me. Nobody cares. I had to drop out of school. Doesn't matter; my classmates just laughed at me anyway. Why won't anybody believe the truth about me? I'm going to have this baby and I'm going to make his world different. You'll see.

Chorus. By your holy cross, you have redeemed the world.

Lector. Lord Jesus, Pilate asked you, "What is truth?"—but he did not listen to the inner voice, his conscience, where truth speaks to every one of us. Jesus, help us to listen. Give us the courage to live in truth. May we offer that truth, and compassion and kindness, to all those with whom we share life. May we see you in their eyes.

Second Station

Roles

Catechist
Lector
Gospel players
- Jesus (nonspeaking role)
- Marcus the Roman Soldier
- Julian the Roman Soldier
- Cassius the Roman Soldier
- Multitude
- Chorus
- Joe
- Jeffrey

Script for the Gospel Drama

[The catechist announces to the group the title of the station to be dramatized.]

Catechist. "Second Station: Jesus Accepts the Cross"

[The catechist describes the Gospel scene to the group.]

Catechist. Under Pilate's command, Jesus is scourged at the pillar with whips. After this degradation, the soldiers pay mock homage to the "King of the Jews." They put a scarlet cloak around his shoulders, shove a reed into his hand to represent a king's scepter, and push down into his scalp a crown of thorns. They encircle him like wild animals, spitting on his face, mocking and degrading him.

[Jesus stands silent in the scarlet cloak, holding the reed and wearing the crown of thorns, as the soldiers circle and taunt him.]

Marcus the Roman Soldier. Hail! King of the Jews! Behold the man!

Julian the Roman Soldier. Still think you're a king, Jesus? Look at the blood running down your face! What kind of king looks like this?

Cassius the Roman Soldier. You can't even see us! The blood is in your eyes.

Marcus. Hey, Your Majesty, your crown is falling . . . We will push it down harder so it never comes off!

Multitude. Crucify! Crucify! Crucify!

Julian. Rip off the scarlet cloak! It's time for the death march.

[Marcus and Cassius try to take the cloak off Jesus.]

Cassius. Stop! This cloak is stuck to his blood and the wounds all over his back. Removing it will tear him. By law, we can't kill him on the street. We have to get him to Golgotha.

Julian. Rip it off him now! *[Marcus and Cassius obey.]* Give him the cross to carry. *[The soldiers heave a heavy wooden cross onto Jesus' shoulder.]* The sun is moving west and he has a long way to walk. Pilate said to be finished before sundown. It's the Law of the Jews. Stupid religious fanatics.

Catechist. Tortured . . . beaten, Jesus is faced with the harsh reality that the walk to Calvary is only beginning. With every step, the weight of the cross cuts deeper into his wounded shoulder. He drags the sorry tree across his battered back, stumbling with each agonizing step. The streets roar with the sounds of jeering as soldiers spit mockery and lewd obscenities in his sacred face. The cruelty pierces his soul. Love personified walks to Golgotha, the place of the skull.

Chorus. By your holy cross, you have redeemed the world.

Catechist. Jesus knows what it feels like to be crushed by humiliation, hurt, and fear. As we face each cross in our own lives, Jesus walks with us through it, comforting us, giving us strength. We can be Christ to one another. With compassion and understanding, we can change one another's lives.

Joe. The guy's a jerk. You know the type: real cool, so important. He's always picking fights with smaller kids. He's like, really cold. This black eye I'm wearing was a present from that bully. I was gonna get my friends together to show him what it feels like to have fists smash your face. But my dad heard me on the phone. Busted!

My dad says this kid's had it rough and I should be the Christian. The guy's got no family, nobody that cares about him. Maybe no one ever really loved or respected him. Dad says when that's the case, a kid doesn't know what to do with all the anger and hurt. He throws his pain on others. Well, he threw a few punches at me, that's for sure. My bruises are going away, but . . . Okay, I'm still afraid that he will beat me up again. But I'm going to try. Today, I'm going to tell him that he packs a real punch and then ask him if he wants to hang out. Maybe we will have lunch. Maybe we will end up friends. It's worth a try.

Jeffrey. The future? Oh, I don't know. I had dreams, once. You know, that pileup with my soccer team changed all that. Yeah, I'm a senior in high school and that freak accident changed everything. I injured my spinal cord in the fall. Now, I'm paralyzed from the neck down. Don't get me wrong. My family really loves me, and my friends are supportive, but some days I don't know how I'm going to get through the rest of my life. I don't know if I want to live. I don't know what to live for. Will you pray for me?

Chorus. By your holy cross, you have redeemed the world.

Lector. Jesus, when you felt you didn't have the strength to face one more step, you called out to your Father and received the grace to go on. In your name, we ask our heavenly Father to nourish our own hearts with courage and peace.

Third Station

Roles

Catechist
Lector
Gospel players
- Pharisee in the Mob
- Sadducee in the Mob
- Multitude
- Cassius the Roman Soldier
- John the Beloved Disciple
- Jesus
- Chorus
- Max
- Mark

Script for the Gospel Drama

[The catechist announces to the group the title of the station to be dramatized.]

Catechist. "Third Station: Jesus Falls the First Time"

[The catechist describes the Gospel scene to the group.]

Catechist. With each step, Jesus' body grows weaker from torture and exhaustion as he walks toward death. The weight of Christ's cross would weary even the strongest human being. Nearing physical collapse, overcome with grief and fatigue, Jesus can't carry the cross one more step. The loss of the blood that pours down his sacred face has drained him of his last reserves of energy. He falls hard on the sharp stones of the road to Golgotha.

Pharisee in the Mob. You called yourself the Son of God! Well, has God ever disowned you now! You're no Son of God. You're just a failure! A freak! A fraud!

Sadducee in the Mob. Serves you right! You're a lesson to those who won't follow the rules! When they see what happens to you, they'll respect the law.

Pharisee. If his disciples could see him now . . . "Follow me," he used to tell them. What a joke! Look how he's tripping on his robes, like a repulsive old drunken fool.

Multitude. King of the Jews! Hail, King of the Jews! We have no king but Caesar! Crucify him! Crucify him! Crucify him!

Cassius the Roman Soldier. Move it, royal charlatan! Listen to your followers shriek. These screaming crowds are hurting my ears. You've got a long way to go, loser! *[Beating Jesus with a whip]* Galilean, I'll whip you till you understand that *you have . . . to go . . . faster.*

John the Beloved Disciple. Stop hurting him! Can't you see he's falling?!

Jesus. *[Stumbling to his knees]* Father, help me . . . The weight is too great. It's crushing me. I can't go on. Look at me . . . How can I go on? Their hatred will not break me. For love of them, I'll carry this cross.

Chorus. By your holy cross, you have redeemed the world.

Catechist. Jesus knows the embarrassment of being too weak to stay up on his feet throughout a difficult journey. He collapses from the sheer weight of the tree, from the fragile reality of human limitation. Resolute in his decision to finish his mission, he steels his will to pull himself back up. Even in his agony, Jesus models and teaches true human greatness—getting up after a fall. With the love of Christ, we too can find the strength to recover from our failures and try again.

Max. You don't walk the streets around here. Not late at night. This is the inner city. Drive-by shootings, drug deals, and gang warfare are common. Gunshots can riddle a car or a house any time of the day. I've tried to stay clean for so long. I watch my back. I stay to myself. But last Saturday night, I was hanging with the gang. I just wanted to be with the guys, but something happened. Everything just exploded. Somebody got really hurt. I didn't want that. I feel so sick inside. Now they're talkin' like I'm in . . . like they're pullin' me in deeper. It's a spider's web. God, help me to rise up out of this mess.

Mark. I don't know what came over me. I just took it. I stole a radio from a store. I don't really know why. I have a radio, a CD player, a stereo . . . I have plenty of money. My parents are rich, they're loaded really. Cars, a big house, a boat. They're always traveling somewhere exotic. They're in Bali, right now. They're going to find out . . . I was arrested for shoplifting. They're not going to like it. They're going to be mad. I don't think they really care, though . . . I mean, about me. They're really involved all the time with their business.

I know it was wrong. It was something that didn't feel good after I got back home. I went to confession. You know—reconciliation. Father Joe was really cool. He didn't yell at me or anything. He said I would have to think about why I did this. I don't want to do it again. Father Joe said that God would help me to get back on track and to deal with my sadness in a healthier way.

Chorus. By your holy cross, you have redeemed the world.

Lector. Jesus, sometimes life's challenges push in on us and test us to the limit. But you fell before us and picked yourself up, to show us that true love never quits. Help us to love ourselves and to love the others in our lives, so that we too will never stop picking ourselves up when we fall.

Fourth Station

Roles

Catechist
Lector
Gospel players
- Joanna the Wife of Chuza
- Mary the Mother of Jesus
- Mary of Magdala
- Mary the Mother of James and Joseph
- Julian the Roman Soldier
- Susanna
- Jesus
- Chorus
- Patty
- Maureen

Script for the Gospel Drama

[The catechist announces to the group the title of the station to be dramatized.]

Catechist. "Fourth Station: Jesus Meets His Sorrowful Mother"

[The catechist describes the Gospel scene to the group.]

Catechist. Mary is a mother. Like human mothers everywhere, she considers her child's happiness and safety vital to her own. On this sad day, she is one in the crowd following her Son on the way to Golgotha. The horror of watching her grown child tortured—enduring senseless agony at the hands of others—is unimaginable. The sword of affliction stabs through this mother's heart in unbearable grief, but she will not leave her Son. In desperation—longing to comfort him, to sooth his wounds, to save him—Mary is powerless to stop the travesty of the cross. But she keeps watch with him, walking every step of the way to Calvary beside him. She is a mother, eternally bonded to her only child.

Joanna the Wife of Chuza. Mary, you're falling. Lean on us, we will help you walk.

Mary the Mother of Jesus. I can't save him; I can't save my Son!

Mary of Magdala. Mary, we're here . . .

Mary the Mother of Jesus. My Son. A trail of precious blood across the cold stone. Footprints in blood . . . I remember his little feet running through streams, running in to bring me a flower with a kiss. Now, these bloodstained footprints . . .

Mary the Mother of James and Joseph. We won't leave him. We will stay close to Jesus to the last. We have to keep up, Mary. One step in front of the other, one step in front of the other.

Mary the Mother of Jesus. I remember teaching him to walk when he was little . . . I love him so much. How could this be happening?

Julian the Roman Soldier. Move back, woman!

Susanna. It's his mother. Leave her alone.

Julian. Look, everyone! It's the *mother* of the King of the Jews. Woman, if you'd reared him to respect the Law and order, he wouldn't now be in our hands.

Mary the Mother of Jesus. Jesus!

Jesus. Mother, look away.

Mary the Mother of Jesus. I will never look away. I will never look away. I am with you to the end.

Jesus. I love you.

Mary the Mother of Jesus. Child of mine, I love you. My Son, my Lord, my God . . . I love you. I love you.

Chorus. By your holy cross, you have redeemed the world.

Catechist. Mary of Nazareth shared the torment inflicted on her Jesus, and endured a mother's martyrdom. The Passion of her Son was a sword that the old prophet Simeon had prophesied would pierce her heart. Mary lovingly gathers to her heart every mother who aches to save her child.

Patty. Hospitals, feeding tubes, shots, tests, lying awake through the dark nights. My little girl is dying and I can't save her. We can't find a bone marrow donor whose tissue is a match for hers. We're running out of time. If we don't find one fast, she will die of leukemia. I feel so alone and helpless. My world is ripping apart. I love this child so much. Pray for my child, please.

Maureen. I don't know what I'm going to do. I can't bear watching this. They're hungry. *"Mommy, when is dinner?"* Three little children . . . pulling at my dress. I want to be a good mother to them. Their shoes are too tight, and this house is too cold. I haven't eaten yet today, but we have to save the food for the little ones. My babies are hungry and we don't have enough food. They need to eat. Their little bodies are growing. Their future health depends on my nourishing them properly. We need money, but where will it come from? Where is a guardian angel when I need one? Please help us, please pray for us.

Chorus. By your holy cross, you have redeemed the world.

Lector. Mary, when you look into the faces of the grieving, the sick, the oppressed, the poor, the unwanted, the hungry . . . you look once again into that beloved face that you followed on the way to Calvary. You have compassion for every hurting man, woman, and child, just as you sorrowed for Jesus. Teach us each to become like a good mother who instinctively reaches out to heal, comfort, and care for others. When we feed the hungry, care for the sick, and show love and mercy to one another, we offer it to your Son.

Fifth Station

Roles

Catechist
Lector
Gospel players
  - Julian the Roman Soldier
  - Marcus the Roman Soldier
  - Aaron, a Teenager in the Crowd
  - Simon of Cyrene
  - Jesus
  - Chorus
  - Molly
  - George

Script for the Gospel Drama

[The catechist announces to the group the title of the station to be dramatized.]

Catechist. "Fifth Station: Simon of Cyrene Helps Jesus Carry His Cross"

[The catechist describes the Gospel scene to the group.]

Catechist. The cross is killing Jesus before he even sets foot on the soil of Calvary. The soldiers insist Jesus must be kept alive for his execution. They have no choice but to select a man from the crowd to help Jesus shoulder the weight of the cross. Simon of Cyrene is volunteered for a role he wants no part of. The destiny of this unlikely circumstance will change Simon in ways he could never have imagined.

Julian the Roman Soldier. For a king, he looks like a clown. Look how he's teetering all over the mud, dragging the cross. At this point, we might as well crucify him right here on the street.

Marcus the Roman Soldier. Our orders were to get him up to Calvary, so people all over the city can watch his death. He is a public criminal.

Aaron, a Teenager in the Crowd. This is too cruel! Someone help him! I'll help him!

Julian. Get back! We need a big, tall, stocky worker . . . Hey, you! Cyrenian! Yeah, you! Get over here! We need someone powerful to help get this cross up the hill.

Simon of Cyrene. Don't look at me! I don't even know this man!

Marcus. You do now. Pick him up and help him with his load.

Simon. No, not me! I'm just minding my own business. You could take anybody in this crowd. Look around; there are hundreds of others who could help him.

Julian. Someone's got to help this criminal, and it isn't going to be us.

Simon. Let go of me! I've never done anything like this before . . . I don't have the time . . . What will people think? What if I lose my reputation?

Marcus. You'll lose more than your reputation if you give us any more excuses. Get on with it, or you'll never see Cyrene again.

Simon. Why me? This is making me sick. This man is filthy, he smells of death, he's a mess. He's guilty, isn't he? Why should I help him carry his cross? Who is this man?

Jesus. *[Calmly, looking into Simon's eyes]* If you give me your time, Simon, I will give you my eternity.

Simon. *[Meeting Jesus' gaze and considering his words]* Poor, dear man. You really do need help, don't you? I will walk with you. Why not me?

Jesus. If you walk this road with me, it will lead us both to glory.

Simon. Lean on me. I've got you. I will follow you to the end.

Chorus. By your holy cross, you have redeemed the world.

Catechist. Those who volunteer to help others often come away feeling like they are the ones who received the gift. Simon of Cyrene was like many individuals who don't want to step out of their comfort zone. But imagine the grace that came over Simon—this one blessed person in human history who helped the Messiah shoulder the weight of redemption on that first Good Friday. We are like the converted and redeemed Simon when we reach out to ease the burden of someone God puts in our path.

Molly. My husband died fifteen years ago. My children call, but they are all so far away. I would love to see my grandchildren. I love my family so much. I don't want to be a burden, so I tell them that I'm happy here, that I'm all right. But the truth is that sometimes the loneliness is terrible. I never thought my old age would be like this. I used to feel like I had purpose, that my life counted. Now I feel like I'm in the way. I remember so much; I could tell such wonderful stories. No one has the time to listen. If only someone would come to visit, or send me a card. If only I could be included in the lives of others.

George. It's been six months since I've had a job. I've taken out a second mortgage on the house, spent my savings, and I'm getting nervous. I have a family to feed, four kids in school. I'm willing to work hard. It's painful to face my children every night, and still have no good news. I love my wife, my kids. I want to take care of them. If someone would only give me a chance, I could do it. I could turn this whole thing around. All I need is a chance.

Chorus. By your holy cross, you have redeemed the world.

Lector. Lord Jesus, help us to see the light as Simon did, and to recognize you in those who struggle with a heavy cross. Give us the grace to be generous, kind, and present to others. Help us to anoint the world with the healing balm of love. And Lord, when life becomes difficult for us, send us one like Simon who can help and can make the burden easier to bear.

Sixth Station

Roles

Catechist
Lector
Gospel players
- Mary the Mother of Jesus
- John the Beloved Disciple
- Salome
- Marcus the Roman Soldier
- Jesus
- Cassius the Roman Soldier
- Chorus
- David
- Stephanie

Script for the Gospel Drama

[The catechist announces to the group the title of the station to be dramatized.]

Catechist. "Sixth Station: Jesus Falls a Second Time"

[The catechist describes the Gospel scene to the group.]

Catechist. Hungry, thirsty, and deprived of sleep, the human Christ is over-whelmed by exhaustion. With his wounds of torture throbbing and screaming to be numbed, the Sacred Heart staggers into a stupor of agony under the inhumane physical, mental, and emotional abuse of the Roman guards. The unending jeers of ridicule, the laughter, anger, and violence break his strength. He is the victim overwhelmed by the abuser as he falls for the second time under the weight of the cross.

Mary the Mother of Jesus. Why do they whip him and force him to go on? Stop beating him, please, please! Oh, Jesus, they are so mean to you . . .

John the Beloved Disciple. We just have to bless him and love him from this distance, Mary. Jesus knew that his mission would lead to his death. We have long killed the prophets. Take comfort, Mary, in the knowledge that your Son so loves the world that nothing can change his will to fulfill his mission of love, even now in this moment.

Salome. I am at a loss to understand how God allows this cruelty to his own Son. What does it mean?

John. God does not will his Son's torture. God wills that we be reconciled to God in love . . . that we be saved. It is humanity who permit and who will Messiah's death. What does this say about us? Jesus chooses to be our Savior. He chooses to accept the Father's will that he be the Anointed One, the Redeemer.

Mary. Old Simeon in the Temple told me that my Son was Messiah, the angel told me that my Son was Messiah. I believe, I believe, but this despair is crushing me.

Marcus the Roman Soldier. It's so hot and stifling. Pass the water, Cassius.

Jesus. One sip . . .

Cassius the Roman Soldier. One kick? Did he say, "One kick"? I'll give you a kick!

Jesus. Father, the weight of the world is too much . . . I am carrying all of them and we're falling, falling . . . fallen . . . *[He once again falls to his knees.]* I don't know if I can carry all these souls. Sins of so many are crushing my heart to despair.

Chorus. By your holy cross, you have redeemed the world.

Catechist. Jesus has walked through the worst hell that humans can inflict on one another. He identifies and weeps with the abused. Jesus understands our pain, our fear, our anxiety and grief. The incarnate Christ has walked through the valley of death to lead you and me into light. He brings compassion, understanding, forgiveness, and healing. When we turn our lives over to the God of love, we can start over on our journey of life.

David. I am a prisoner of conscience in a remote city jail. I was interrogated and imprisoned on trumped-up charges because I spoke out for civil rights. There are so many people suffering in my country because of the corruption in the government. Somebody had to do something. Yes, I knew that they might arrest me. But freedom is more important than any individual. Somebody had to do something and it was me. The guards are cruel; they have no mercy. They keep me hungry and cold. No one can visit me, and the guards badger me to give up my beliefs, with beatings and threats against my family. God, help me to be strong.

Stephanie. I was sexually molested when I was little. I feel so ashamed of this. My counselor told me that the shame does not belong to me, that the shame I feel is the abuser's shame. She said that I was too little to understand, that it is not my fault . . . that grown-ups are supposed to protect children. The person who molested me was very sick. What happened to me was sinful and wrong and against the will of God. Sometimes I think nothing will ever make me feel safe or happy again. But I know that God will help me to find the courage to heal.

I told my father what happened to me. My counselor and my father reported the abuser to the child protection agency. I'm learning that forgiveness means giving the pain to God. What happened to me will never be okay, but I am healing. I'm learning to love myself. None of this was my fault.

Chorus. By your holy cross, you have redeemed the world.

Catechist. God hates all sins of abuse. God cherishes the survivors of abuse and weeps with them. At the same moment, God weeps for the lost human being who is the abuser. No situation is so dark and far gone that God cannot heal it in time. There are no limits to God's love, no limits to God's ability to re-create all of us in the image of the love of Jesus. The healing begins with our choice to seek reconciliation, to seek help, and to change how we see ourselves today and tomorrow.

Lector. Lord and Savior, you fell under the weight of our sins. But our sins did not stop you from getting back up and walking the rest of the way. You refuse to give up on us. We matter to you. Thank you for the sacrifice you made in order to offer us freedom, love, and the chance to begin again as children of God.

Seventh Station

Roles

Catechist
Lector
Gospel players
- Teenage Girl in the Crowd
- Little Boy in the Crowd
- Reuben the Pharisee
- Seraphia the Child
- Veronica
- Jesus (nonspeaking role)
- Julian the Roman Soldier
- Chorus
- Melinda
- Neil

Script for the Gospel Drama

[The catechist announces to the group the title of the station to be dramatized.]

Catechist. "Seventh Station: Veronica Wipes the Face of Jesus"

[The catechist describes the Gospel scene to the group.]

Catechist. Veronica is a heroic figure in the story of Christ's Passion. Her name derives from the words *vera* (true) and *icon* (image). Christ leaves the true image of himself on her veil as a sign of gratitude for her mercy. We don't know if this woman is an actual historical person. But we do know something more important—that she represents those who are unafraid to act from the better side of their nature. Veronica is a woman of conscience, much like those who hid Jewish families from Nazi arrest during World War II. Veronica is a woman of compassion, a kindred spirit to Mother Teresa, who picked up dying beggars from the rodent-infested streets of Calcutta and loved them like family on their deathbed. Veronica is a woman of courage, like the medics and nurses who place themselves between bullets and the victims of war. Veronica loves Jesus. His need is more urgent to her than her own comfort or safety.

Teenage Girl in the Crowd. Is that really the famous Jesus of Nazareth? What happened to his face? I wouldn't even know it was him.

Little Boy in the Crowd. He's all bloody and swollen.

Reuben the Pharisee. The mask has been ripped off. This is the real face of Jesus. It's ugly, isn't it? Hurts the eyes to look at him.

Seraphia the Child. Mother, where are we going? This mob is frightening me.

Veronica. Hold my hand, little one—and don't let go, child. We have to get to the Lord immediately, to comfort him in any way we can.

Seraphia. He looks scary.

Veronica. It's only because he's in so much pain. Remember the time Jesus let you and your friends come to his lap, and he told you stories? Remember the little girl who was so sick, and he reached out and touched her and she was well? Jesus is our friend. We have to stand by him today.

Seraphia. But the soldiers are so mean. What if they hurt us too?

Veronica. Jesus said he would lay down his life for us. The least we can do is reach out to wipe his poor face.

Seraphia. Mother! You are taking off your veil! You may be arrested. Women must cover their heads. It's the law.

Veronica. Some laws are not just. To comfort the suffering is a higher law.

[Veronica wipes the face of the Christ with her linen veil.]

Julian the Roman Soldier. Look! A woman . . . broke through the guards . . . and wiped his wounded face with her veil.

Veronica. Lord Jesus, I hope this will help soothe away the grief.

Julian. Stand back! Out of the way! All of you women are getting too close!

Veronica. Seraphia, stand close to me. I know God will protect us today . . . Jesus! Your poor face! Let me soothe away the grief, the filth that has been spit on your face. I know it's you beneath all this sweat and grime, and you are so beautiful to me.

Julian. Away, woman! Don't touch the man! *[Grabbing her veil]* What is *this* on your veil? . . . He left the image of his face—

Veronica. He left his soul on our hearts. Thank you, Jesus. I will never forget you.

Julian. *[Amazed]* Who is this man?

Veronica. My Lord has left us a precious gift. Now that bloodstained veil is my greatest treasure. For there, pressed in its threads, is the shadow of his face.

Chorus. By your holy cross, you have redeemed the world.

Catechist. The blood and tears and bruises on Jesus' face hid his beauty, but Veronica could see past the wounds and grime. We are called to see the dignity and beauty in every person, for every human being is a child of God. When we have the courage and the compassion to see past the disguise of another person in pain, and reach out to touch that person with love, it is Jesus whom we comfort.

Melinda. I know, you've seen me a hundred times but you don't know my name. Our eyes never meet because when you come by, I look down. I'm ashamed to be homeless. There are thousands just like me in the downtown areas of every large metropolis in this country. We live on the streets, in abandoned buildings, in parks. I wasn't always homeless. I once had a job, a family, respect. Then my life turned crazy for a while, and now I'm on the outside looking in. People are afraid of me and hurry past me, but I'm a human being just like them.

Neil. I was only thirteen years old when those guys almost beat the life out of me. It was just because they didn't like the color of my skin. They had a great time. Made me plead for my life. I was so terrified, so ashamed. The worst part was all those people. They all just stood around watching the attack and didn't do one thing to stop it. I heard this one guy tell his friend: "Don't get involved. There might be a lawsuit." So while Mr. Businessman watched, that mob half killed me. I don't know why they didn't kill me. I'll have these scars for the rest of my life.

Chorus. By your holy cross, you have redeemed the world.

Lector. Jesus, help us always to see your face in the distressing disguise of those who are hurting. Give us the courage of Veronica. Leave the imprint of your own beautiful face on all our acts of thoughtfulness and love.

Eighth Station

Roles

Catechist
Lector
Gospel players
- Multitude
- Rachel
- Ruth
- Miriam
- Rebecca
- Jesus
- Chorus
- Robert
- Cindi

Script for the Gospel Drama

[The catechist announces to the group the title of the station to be dramatized.]

Catechist. "Eighth Station: Jesus Consoles the Women of Jerusalem"

[The catechist describes the Gospel scene to the group.]

Catechist. Many people mourn for Christ on his way of the cross. These unknown sympathizers, the silent majority who are appalled by the scene, long to shout out against the injustice. Women—true to their time and culture—beat their breasts and wail in the midst of this tragedy. Christ feels and blesses every tear. Their compassion does not go unnoticed.

Multitude. King of the Jews! King of the Jews! Let his blood be upon us!

Rachel. He touched my little boy, who was blind, and my boy can see! Now they push thorns in his own eyes. This is madness!

Multitude. Crucify him!

Ruth. Jesus of Nazareth, you had mercy on all people! Where is our mercy for you?!

Miriam. The very stones are screaming out at this injustice!

Rebecca. God, help him! God, help the Holy Man of Nazareth!

Jesus. Women, do not weep for me. Weep for yourselves and for your children. This bitter day will pass, but another bitter one is coming—when you will beg the mountains to fall on you.

Catechist. In 70 C.E., less than forty years after Christ's death, the Romans will sack Jerusalem, crushing the people. In supreme irony, the stone Temple, which the elders revere as untouchable and timeless, will be utterly demolished, whereas the crucified temple of Christ's body will have gloriously risen, to reign for all eternity.

Jesus. Do not despair. You are in my heart. Beyond every injustice of this world, Truth will reign.

Chorus. By your holy cross, you have redeemed the world.

Catechist. Jesus knows the sorrows and worries that await each of us in our lifetime, and he comforts us with the remembrance of his own Passion, which ended miraculously in glory.

Robert. You know why I became a cop? Because of the outrage I feel when I see innocent people—law-abiding women, children, and men—being victimized on the streets. I carry home the image of their faces. Someday I might be the one caught in the cross fire. Or someone I care about may get hurt. We can't just stand by and let these criminals take our streets, our homes. Some of us offer ourselves to protect the safety of others.

Cindi. I never dreamed my mother would have breast cancer. She's such a good woman. She did everything she could for me when I was growing up. So now I'm caring for her during her chemotherapy treatments. But I'm so angry. I just can't stand to see her in pain. I think she's scared. It's not right; she's such a kind and loving person. I know that God doesn't send us these things, but I wish God would stop it. So, cancer runs in my family. I wonder if I could be next. This is a hard cross to bear. Lord, be with me in my fear.

Chorus. By your holy cross, you have redeemed the world.

Lector. Jesus, your compassion is always present. It is a faithful refuge we can always turn to on the journey of our life.

Ninth Station

Roles

Catechist
Lector
Gospel players
- Eli the Pharisee
- Nathan the Sadducee
- Cassius the Roman Soldier
- Salome
- Simon of Cyrene
- Multitude
- Jesus
- Chorus
- Hank
- Cassy

Script for the Gospel Drama

[The catechist announces to the group the title of the station to be dramatized.]

Catechist. "Ninth Station: Jesus Falls a Third Time"

[The catechist describes the Gospel scene to the group.]

Catechist. Jesus staggers and falls again. He is Messiah, Son of God, Anointed One, Chosen One, and yet he walks the road of a common criminal, a social outcast, an exile. How did this atrocity happen? It happened because of the sins and weaknesses of ordinary people all around him . . . the greed of Judas . . . the envy of the chief priests . . . the fear of the crowds who sought to appease unpredictable authorities . . . the callous indifference of Pilate.

Eli the Pharisee. What a joke! This is the Miracle Man who helped the lame to walk?

Nathan the Sadducee. Helped the lame to walk, the deaf to hear, the blind to see. Now he's the one who is lame and deaf and blind. Ha!

Cassius the Roman Soldier. Shove the man, push him; just get him up the hill! I don't want to make a whole career out of this crucifixion. Hurry it up!

Salome. Bullies!

Simon of Cyrene. Lean on me, Jesus. This hill is steep. I'm right behind you. If you fall, we fall together.

Multitude. Death to the "Prophet"! Crucify the "King"!

Cassius. Yank him! Get him up this hill!

Jesus. Please don't pull me! Simon, we're falling! *[Jesus and Simon collapse under the weight of the cross.]*

Chorus. By your holy cross, you have redeemed the world.

Catechist. Suffering continues in our world because of the same sins and weaknesses found in Judas, in the chief priests, in the mob who chose Barabbas, and in Pilate.

Hank. They jumped me for no reason. I was on the way to my car in my bank's parking lot when they mugged me. They wanted money. I guess they were drug addicts or something. I don't know. The police haven't caught them yet. They're still out there and I'm afraid they'll do it again to somebody else. They only got thirty dollars, and I got a bullet in my side. The doctors worked for six hours to stop the bleeding and save my life. Thirty dollars. Isn't my life worth more than thirty dollars? Jesus understands; he was betrayed for thirty pieces of silver.

Cassy. I've tried to make friends. But I don't think anybody really likes me. The girls at school act like I'm not good enough to hang out with them. They're really mean, say rude things, call me names. I tried to invite some of them over after school. You know, so we could get to know one another. They just laughed. Maybe I'm not pretty enough. Maybe my grades aren't the best. Maybe my parents don't make enough money. I don't know. It's hard to be alone. I wish somebody would care.

Chorus. By your holy cross, you have redeemed the world.

Lector. Jesus, your falling steps on the way to Calvary were set into motion by all kinds of forces. Help us to understand that we all can fall—into sin, into confusion, into despair—through greed, envy, fear, and indifference. Help us to be your light in the world. When we see injustice or cruelty, help us to respond in love.

Tenth Station

Roles

Catechist
Lector
Gospel players
- Julian the Roman Soldier
- Simon of Cyrene
- Cassius the Roman Soldier
- Multitude
- Marcus the Roman Soldier
- Joanna the Wife of Chuza
- Susanna
- Mary the Mother of Jesus
- Pharisee in the Crowd
- Chorus
- Brian
- Elizabeth

Script for the Gospel Drama

[The catechist announces to the group the title of the station to be dramatized.]

Catechist. "Tenth Station: Jesus Is Stripped of His Garments"

[The catechist describes the Gospel scene to the group.]

Catechist. At the highest point of Calvary's rocky height, visible to onlookers across Jerusalem, Jesus braces himself for public execution. The soldiers rip the clothes from his wasted body, leaving him completely exposed to the elements and scornful eyes. Soon he will hang on his cross—in full view of both enemies and loved ones—as a naked, bleeding man, stripped of all dignity.

Julian the Roman Soldier. Move out of the way, Cyrenian. Your time with the King of the Jews is over.

Simon of Cyrene. Simon, my name is Simon. Please, stop hurting him! I helped him get his body up this hill. He can't take anymore!

Cassius the Roman Soldier. Want to hang on the cross for him? We have orders. Get out of our way.

Multitude. King of the Jews! Where's your power now?!

Marcus the Roman Soldier. Strip him!

Julian. *[Trying to do as ordered]* His robe won't tear!

Marcus. Hold on to him. Cassius and I will work off this crown of thorns, then you other soldiers yank the garment over his head. *[The soldiers strip Jesus of his crown and robe.]*

Joanna the Wife of Chuza. His mother made that robe for him . . . every woven thread touched with so much love. They handle it like a filthy rag.

Susanna. Look how they treat him, like an old carcass, like trash.

Mary the Mother of Jesus. Oh, my Son . . . your precious body . . . what have they done to you?!

Pharisee in the Crowd. So it all comes down to this. The "Holy One," the "Kingly One," is as ordinary as a crushed thistle in the dirt. He's a nothing. And he's got nowhere to hide! Everyone in Jerusalem with eyes can look up to this hill and see that the charade is over. Caiaphas was right. The Messiah act was pure fraud. He wasn't even a good rabbi. His own friends left him in the end. I like that it all caught up with him. Now we know we were right.

Chorus. By your holy cross, you have redeemed the world.

Catechist. By taking human flesh, Jesus, the Son of God, has made himself vulnerable—but never more so than on this day as he is stripped naked and crucified. He understands the pain of exposure, the embarrassment of losing the respect of others. When a person or a situation strips us of our dignity, Jesus is very close to us. He experienced that terrible feeling himself.

Brian. I flunked. They told me this afternoon. So I either drop out or repeat senior year. My English lit teacher and the principal called me in for a meeting. My body felt cold as I heard them saying I wouldn't graduate with my friends. It's always been this way for me. Learning disabled, they call me. This learning disability has been a weight on me my whole life. Everyone's so excited about graduation. I feel left out and sad. It hurts to fail.

Elizabeth. It was a stroke. Joseph was teaching when it happened. You'd love him. He's brilliant. He has three advanced degrees and has taught at the university for fifteen years. It was during a class on ancient Egypt . . . All of a sudden, his muscles wouldn't work and he collapsed in a heap on the classroom floor. One minute I was listening to my brother in an exhilarating debate with his students, and the next he was lying on the floor unable move. Now he has to learn how to speak all over again, like a baby. Everything he was has been stripped away. I know that if anyone can recover, he can. But Joseph says that he feels naked and useless.

Chorus. By your holy cross, you have redeemed the world.

Lector. Lord, when our dignity and our gifts seem stripped away, you tell us that you cherish us for the very one we are. Our value in your eyes is beyond all understanding.

Eleventh Station

Roles

Catechist
Lector
Gospel players
- Cassius the Roman Soldier
- Salome
- Marcus the Roman Soldier
- Multitude
- Mary of Magdala
- Mary the Mother of Jesus
- Jesus
- John the Beloved Disciple
- Mary the Mother of James and John
- Mary the Mother of James and Joseph
- Chorus
- Baby Doe
- Nicholas

Script for the Gospel Drama

[The catechist announces to the group the title of the station to be dramatized.]

Catechist. "Eleventh Station: Jesus Is Nailed to the Cross"

[The catechist describes the Gospel scene to the group.]

Catechist. Five-inch-long spikes pierce Christ's flesh as soldiers drive them through his wrists and feet. They pin him to the altar that is his cross. Waves of excruciating agony crash over him. It is too late to turn back. He cries out to his Father with the anguish of a child in terror: *"Abba! [Daddy!] Where are you? I'm so alone and afraid. Why have you forsaken me?"*

Cassius the Roman Soldier. The "throne" is ready for the "King." Lay him on it and pin down his arms and legs.

Salome. God, help him. Oh, dear God, help him.

Marcus the Roman Soldier. *[Brandishing a hammer and nails]* Hold his wrist to the wood. I'll pound.

Multitude. Crucify him!

Mary of Magdala. Oh, Beloved One, my heart is nailed to the cross with you. They don't know who you are.

Marcus. He's going crazy with the pain. Hold him down. Keep the other wrist steady while I pound the nail through it.

Mary the Mother of Jesus. All at once, in my mind, he's little. Playing with wood in Joseph's shop. *"Oh, Jesus, did the nail slip and pierce your little hand? Let Mommy hold you and kiss the pain away."* My Son, my Son!

Jesus. *I thirst.*

John the Beloved Disciple. "I thirst." I just heard him say, "I thirst." Some- one give him something to drink!

Mary the Mother of James and John. *[Holding out a flask or jar]* I carried some spiced wine for him, John.

John. Guard, please . . . he's dying. Will you give him this spiced wine?

Cassius. Wine looks good, but not for the prisoner. He will get a sponge soaked with vinegar.

[Cassius offers Jesus the sponge, but Jesus will not take it.]

Mary the Mother of James and Joseph. He refuses the vinegar, even though it might dull the pain. Jesus doesn't want to be drugged. Even now, he prays.

Jesus. *Father, I love you! Why have you forsaken me?*

Chorus. By your holy cross, you have redeemed the world.

Catechist. Nailed to the cross, Jesus is a helpless human being, utterly unable to escape his sorrow. Spiritually, he is going through the dark night of the soul—a sense of complete abandonment and deep despair.

Baby Doe. Life. I'm so excited to be alive. God has dreamed such plans for me. I'm going to make my parents so happy. I'm a strong, healthy baby boy, growing day by day. My heart and all the organs in my body are perfect. My eyes are green and I look like my mommy. I'm an unborn child, wrapped in the safe, warm waters of my mother's womb. I think I have a gift for music. The constant rhythm of Mommy's heartbeat and the melody of her voice are my first song. I love my mother.

Oh, no, what is wrong with Mommy? Why is she sobbing? Her heart's beating too fast and so is mine! What is that sharp, piercing, stabbing pain? It's hurting me. It's killing me!

Nicholas. AIDS kills you one day at a time. Oh, yes, it's a slow death. My body is covered with sores and the fevers rage. But that's not the worst of it. I could handle the pain, the constant weakness and nausea, but the abandonment by my family is what is really killing me. My parents don't want to have anything to do with me. My brother say he's ashamed of me. I'm a big disappointment to them, a disgrace. Medical people monitor my vital signs, but avoid touching me. I had friends once, but they've all stopped coming. They've all forsaken me and I'm so alone. This must be how Jesus felt when people turned on him and ran away as he faced death.

Chorus. By your holy cross, you have redeemed the world.

Lector. Jesus, the nails that held you fast to your cross were instruments of evil, and the wounds they left stayed with you even in your resurrected glory. Help us to understand that the nails and sharp hurts that challenge us in our life can be transformed into treasures of redemption if we unite them with your sacrifice, and bear them with the help of your grace.

Twelfth Station

Roles

Catechist
Lector
Gospel players

- Zacchaeus the Believer
- John the Beloved Disciple
- Multitude
- Thief on the Left
- Dismas, the Thief on the Right
- Jesus
- Mary the Mother of Jesus
- Mary of Magdala (nonspeaking role)
- Joanna the Wife of Chuza (nonspeaking role)
- Mary the Wife of Clopas (nonspeaking role)
- Elias the Pharisee
- Joseph of Arimathea
- Julian the Roman Soldier
- Marcus the Roman Soldier
- Chorus
- Cecilia
- Jack

Script for the Gospel Drama

[The catechist announces to the group the title of the station to be dramatized.]

Catechist. "Twelfth Station: Jesus Dies on the Cross"

[The catechist describes the Gospel scene to the group.]

Catechist. For three hours, Jesus hangs on the cross, each minute dragging on like a wicked eternity. Two thieves hang to his right and his left. One thief curses his lot. The second is so intrigued with the peace and innocence of Jesus that his heart is transformed. Jesus begs the Father to forgive all his own persecutors. And he takes care of his mother by entrusting her to his friend John. To the end, Jesus personifies a mercy and pure love that no evil can begin to touch.

Zacchaeus the Believer. The day I met the Lord, I climbed up in a tree so I could see him better. He told me to come down. Now he is up on a tree looking down at me. I would give anything if I could reach up and carry him home. We have to save him, John, but how?

John the Beloved Disciple. I love him too, Zacchaeus. I don't want to lose the Master, but he warned us this would happen. I remember when he talked to us about it, just a few nights ago. He said that unless a grain of wheat falls to the ground and dies, it cannot bear fruit. But why does he have to die this way? Something has gone very wrong.

Multitude. You saved others! Now save yourself!

Thief on the Left. Why should this guy in the middle be saved? Why is everyone paying him all the attention? I should be saved! I had good reasons for my crimes.

Dismas, the Thief on the Right. No, you didn't, and neither did I. We hurt people. We deserve to hang. But this man beside us is different. He's done no wrong. They yell and spit on him with hatred, but he prays for them. I can hear him praying. His peacefulness is a miracle. He makes me wish I had been a better man.

Jesus. Dismas, this very day, you will be with me in Paradise.

Mary the Mother of Jesus. Jesus, my Son, I love you so much. Joseph loved you so much. You were the greatest joy in my whole life. Your death crushes me.

Jesus. Mother, behold your Son. I love you. I want you to take John into your heart as a son now. John, please love my mother as your own. Take care of her for me. We are family now and always.

Mary the Mother of Jesus. All of us who stand by him are family forever. Look at us . . . Zacchaeus, you were the chief tax collector in Jericho . . . Magdala, you were a woman of the streets of Jerusalem . . . Joanna, you are the wife of King Herod's steward . . . Beloved sister Mary, wife of Clopas, you believed Jesus was the One from the moment I told you the angel came to me . . . Joseph of Arimathea, you are a member of the Sanhedrin, yet a secret believer who followed him to this hill . . . I was a simple girl from Nazareth, and God put him in my womb so he could be born for all of us.

John. Mary, you are the mother of all of us now, and all those who will come.

Elias the Pharisee. Hey, Jesus, you claimed you would destroy the Temple and then rebuild it. You lied! Our Temple stands! We were right and you were wrong. Now you die!

Joseph of Arimathea. The words of Isaiah keep coming to me. I memorized them at that very Temple when I was only a child:

> He was spurned and avoided by men, a man of suffering, accustomed to infirmity . . . and we held him in no esteem.
>
> Yet it was our infirmities that he bore, our sufferings that he endured, while we thought of him as stricken, as one smitten by God and afflicted. But he was pierced for our offenses, crushed for our sins; upon him was the chastisement that makes him whole; by his stripes we were healed. We had all gone astray like sheep, each following our own way, but the Lord laid upon him the guilt of us all.

> He is the One sent for love of us. Why can't they see who he is?

Multitude. Impostor! False king! Failure!

Julian the Roman Soldier. The sky is getting so dark. Storm clouds shroud the light. It's almost eerie.

Marcus the Roman Soldier. If he doesn't die soon, we will break his legs. Let's gamble for his robe. Pass the wine.

Jesus. *Father, forgive them, for they do not realize what they are doing.*

Joseph. It is Passover, and tonight they kill the paschal lamb. They don't even realize that they are killing the real Lamb. He is the Just One foretold by Isaiah: "Though he was harshly treated, he submitted and opened not his mouth; like a lamb led to the slaughter or a sheep before the shearers, he was silent and opened not his mouth."

Chorus. The angel of death said: "When I see the blood of the lamb, I will pass over the houses of the Israelites. They shall be freed. They shall be saved."

Jesus. *Father . . . into your hands . . . I commend . . . my spirit . . .*

Mary the Mother of Jesus. My Son! I love you forever!

Jesus. *It . . . is . . . finished.*

Chorus. By your holy cross, you have redeemed the world.

Catechist. According to Gospel accounts, darkness has covered the earth during the hours Christ has hung on the cross. At the moment of his death, a violent earthquake rocks the earth, and stones split in half. A Roman centurion, filled with awe at the rupture of nature, says in fear, "Surely this man was the Son of God." Signs are everywhere. The veil in the Temple is ripped from top to bottom. Graves open and bodies arise out of them, and holy people who have died are seen by many in Jerusalem. During this cataclysmic break in time, death and darkness seem to dominate. But just as at the dawn of Creation, the Spirit of God hovers over the chaos.

Cecilia. She was my only daughter. Sally was seventeen years old, and so full of laughter, intelligence, and dreams when that drunk driver hit her. She was walking home from school. He was speeding and didn't even know he had hit her. He killed my little girl. She was the greatest gift God ever gave me. I still love her so much. I can't believe that she's gone. Why did she have to *be* in *that place* at *that time?* We have always been such a prayerful family. I can't begin to imagine why God allowed this! I know how the sorrowful mother Mary felt when they killed her Son.

Jack. She was only thirty. The virus attacked her heart. My wife died in my arms in the hospital. I never loved anyone in my life as much as I loved her. Why was she taken from me so soon? We had so many plans for the future. So many dreams . . . I hoped for children . . . grandchildren. I hate to come home at night because the house feels so empty. I can't imagine the rest of my life without her. This grief is breaking my heart.

Chorus. By your holy cross, you have redeemed the world.

Lector. Jesus, you poured out from the chalice of your body an atoning torrent of precious blood. To your dying breath, you lived your life for love of us. You are the Light of the World. Although suffering is not your Father's will, help us to understand that all our griefs can have purpose and value if we freely unite them with the sufferings of your Passion.

Thirteenth Station

Roles

Catechist
Lector
Gospel players
- Mary the Mother of Jesus
- Jesus (nonspeaking role)
- Mary the Wife of Clopas
- Mary of Magdala
- Joanna the Wife of Chuza
- Susanna
- John the Beloved Disciple
- Martha
- Chorus
- Margaret
- Adam

Script for the Gospel Drama

[The catechist announces to the group the title of the station to be dramatized.]

Catechist. "Thirteenth Station: Jesus Is Taken Down from the Cross"

[The catechist describes the Gospel scene to the group.]

Catechist. The public drama of Christ's Passion is complete. The Gospel of John notes symbolic details that speak to Christ's sacrificial role as the Lamb of God. Like the Passover lamb, Jesus does not suffer broken bones, but is pierced in the side after death, and blood and water pour forth.

The jeering mob, satisfied, slips away. Only the ones who love him remain. Silently they take down the Lord's lifeless body from the cross and lay it in the arms of his anguished mother. The body that God knit in her womb embraces death. The face that she loves is swollen and battered beyond recognition. The eyes are lifeless. His body is cold and limp. Mary grasps her dead Son to her heart and weeps. Her grief is beyond words.

Mary the Mother of Jesus. *[Holding the dead Jesus]* They put a sword through his heart. King Herod wanted to do that when he was just a baby.

Mary the Wife of Clopas. You escaped to Egypt to save him.

Mary the Mother of Jesus. The sword caught up with us.

Mary of Magdala. It's over. All hope is lost.

Joanna the Wife of Chuza. We need to trust him. He promised us that he was Messiah, the Christ, the Light of the World.

Susanna. But he's dead. What do we have to hold on to?

John the Beloved Disciple. We have his word. He said, "I am the Resurrection and the life."

Mary the Mother of Jesus. He was born of my womb, but it was he who gave me life.

John. Mary, his life changed all of us. The world will never be the same.

Martha. None of us will ever stop loving him.

Susanna. But without him, the light's gone out of the world.

Mary of Magdala. It's so dark and empty. I died with him. It's over.

Chorus. By your holy cross, you have redeemed the world.

Catechist. When we are hit by a disaster, such as the senseless death of a loved one, it can be hard to find any light in the darkness. On the first Good Friday, the friends of Jesus hold hands through a tragedy that leaves them lost and desolate.

Margaret. I want back my son—flesh of my flesh, child of my heart—not some medal for bravery in a conflict I don't even understand. They put a flag in my arms. A flag . . . cold comfort for a mother's broken heart. I stand and watch the honors of a military funeral—taps and a gun salute for the soldier I call son. None of it makes any sense to me. I will never get over this loss. My son is dead.

Adam. I'm only sixteen. When you're a sixteen-year-old guy, you need your dad. We have always been so close. I was at a party the night it happened. When I got home, there were police, bright lights, and paramedics all over the street. People were screaming. Then the bottom dropped out of my stomach. The police were at my front door, talking to my mother. Her eyes were all red and she just grabbed me and started sobbing. I heard someone in the crowd say, "He was shot." It was my dad who was shot. The robber broke into our house and killed my dad. He was trying to protect Mom. The robber just killed him. He killed my dad. Why didn't God stop this? Life looks dark and ugly now.

Chorus. By your holy cross, you have redeemed the world.

Lector. Lord Jesus, you grieve with us in the chaos and fear of our lives. And though it appears that the powers of darkness can be invincible, you have conquered death. Salvation is at hand. During the darkest moments of our lives, help us to trust in you completely.

Fourteenth Station

Roles

Catechist
Lector
Gospel players
- Joseph of Arimathea
- John the Beloved Disciple
- Nicodemus
- Jesus (nonspeaking role)
- Mary of Magdala
- Mary the Mother of Jesus
- Pontius Pilate
- High Priest Annas
- High Priest Caiaphas
- Chorus
- Sharon
- Josh

Script for the Gospel Drama

[The catechist announces to the group the title of the station to be dramatized.]

Catechist. "Fourteenth Station: Jesus Is Laid in the Tomb"

[The catechist describes the Gospel scene to the group.]

Catechist. It is Jewish custom to bury a body before sundown on the day of death. Jesus has died on a Friday afternoon, with the holy day of the Sabbath quickly approaching. His burial is all the more urgent because the Law of Moses decrees that leaving a crucified criminal to hang overnight will defile the land.

All four Gospels speak of a man named Joseph of Arimathea who handles the responsibility of Jesus' burial. He is a rich member of the Sanhedrin, the Jewish council that turned Jesus over to Pilate. In contrast to his colleagues, Joseph was a secret follower of Jesus. And he was courageous enough to ask Pilate for permission to take the body of Jesus for a proper Jewish burial.

Joseph of Arimathea. John, I'm here to help. Pilate gave me permission to take the Lord's body for burial. I have a tomb waiting.

John the Beloved Disciple. Thank God you've come, Joseph. We have to act fast. All of us here are ready to help take the Lord's body to his resting place. Nicodemus, do you know Joseph?

Nicodemus. I have heard of you, Joseph. We both came to see Jesus by night. Our love for him makes us brothers. Jesus promised me that everyone who believes in him will not perish, but will have eternal life. I'm holding on to that. I am forever in his debt.

[Nicodemus and Joseph pick up the dead Jesus and walk toward the waiting tomb, followed by John, Mary of Magdala, and Mary the Mother of Jesus.]

Mary of Magdala. Yes, everything about him was so generous. I was so grateful to find his love that one night I wept, and washed his feet with my tears. He told everyone in the room that I was anointing him for his burial. I've dreaded since that night that something like this would happen. What a bad dream it is to lay my loved one in a tomb.

Mary the Mother of Jesus. Your sorrow is as great as your love, Mary. My Son was blessed to have your friendship while he lived.

Joseph. Our procession will stop at that rock. The tomb is just inside. We have just enough time to wrap the Lord's body in the burial linen.

Mary the Mother of Jesus. I remember the night I laid him in a manger and wrapped him in swaddling clothes. Now I lay him in a tomb, wrapped in a shroud.

Catechist. Meanwhile, the high priests and Pharisees pay a visit to Pilate. They are concerned about Jesus' burial too, but for very different reasons.

Pontius Pilate. What is it now?

High Priest Annas. Governor, we demand that Jesus' body be watched.

Pilate. My soldiers assured me he's dead. What harm can he be to you dead?

High Priest Caiaphas. Oh, we think he could be even more dangerous after his death.

Pilate. The man won't be preaching from a tomb!

Annas. Rumors are circulating that he claimed he will rise after three days. His followers could steal his body and claim he is alive!

Caiaphas. A cult could arise. This Jesus business could go on for another ten years!

Pilate. Well, we wouldn't want that. I'll allow guards at the entrance of the tomb so this whole matter ends cleanly once and for all. Jesus of Nazareth is dead. With my authority, I have decreed it!

Chorus. By your holy cross, you have redeemed the world.

Catechist. In the darkness and silence of the tomb, Jesus lies dead. In the natural order of things, hope seems crushed. Desolation and anguish cloud the hearts of his friends. What could possibly restore their joy?

Sharon. When I first held my baby daughter in my arms, I was filled with dreams for her future. But little Sally was born with a severe birth defect that affects her greatly. I have such shame, because her condition was caused by my taking drugs and alcohol when I was pregnant. Our lives are going to be very different from what I expected. I love my little girl, but I'm afraid I'm not up to the challenges we will face together in all the years ahead. God, please help me. Forgive me for my foolishness and give me the strength to be a good mother, to help my little girl to live up to her full potential.

Josh. My parents used to fight a lot, but at least we were all together. Ever since the divorce, I don't feel completely at home anywhere. I feel torn in half. When I'm with my dad and his new family, I miss my mom. When Mom and I are together, I miss Dad. When they complain and say horrible things about each other, I think that there must be something wrong with me. Well, I am half my mom and half my dad. I guess marriage and family just don't work anymore. How can I ever trust in love again? It's so unpredictable. The world is full of disappointments. No one knows how alone and depressed I really feel about my life.

Chorus. By your holy cross, you have redeemed the world.

Lector. Jesus, you cherish us even with all our sins and human baggage. If we ever feel unloved or unwanted, we have only to look at a crucifix and remember that you love us with a love past all understanding. Every trial and difficulty, every regret and sorrow and cross can be transformed into something full of hope and beauty if we reach out for you and trust you. When we feel buried in our problems, you lovingly work out a plan for us that will one day be revealed.

Follow-up After the Drama
(See resource intro–A, "Leader's Tasks.")

Reflection Questions

- If you had lived in the city of Jerusalem on the day of Christ's death, how do you think you would have reacted?
- Those who condemned Jesus eventually had to stand before him "to be judged." So will every one of us. What would you like your life story to look like by the time you stand before Christ as your Judge?

- Jesus was fully human as well as divine. What emotions do you think he may have experienced during his betrayal, his arrest, his interrogation, and his Passion, and at the moment of his death? Do you understand that Jesus has experienced all of the human emotions that you do?
- Human beings can choose to act out of their dark side or out of a grace-filled heart. Consider the weaknesses and motives that may have been at work in the behavior of these people:
  - Judas
  - the chief priests
  - Pontius Pilate
  - the thief on the left
  - the Roman soldiers

    Now consider the traits, inspirations, and motives that may have influenced the behavior of these people:
  - the holy women on the way of the cross
  - Veronica
  - Dismas, the thief on the right
  - John the Beloved Disciple
  - Joseph of Arimathea
- Suffering is a mystery. We know that our loving God never sends pain and suffering to us. And yet, strangely, God is present in our crosses, leading and comforting us, drawing us closer to the Divine Heart. How can we more fully offer our times of trial to our Lord?

Improv
(See resource intro–A, "Leader's Tasks.")

Closure
(See resource intro–A, "Leader's Tasks.")

Holy Saturday Icon

He is risen! Alleluia! But where is he? The Living Jesus is found in the flame of love that burns in the hearts of all people and throughout all creation.
A: Matthew 28:1–10; B: Mark 16:1–8; C: Luke 24:1–12

Holy Saturday and Easter Sunday

Gospel Readings and Themes

Holy Saturday

Cycle A. Matthew 28:1–10. Go tell the brothers. He is risen!
Cycle B. Mark 16:1–8. Who rolled back the stone?
Cycle C. Luke 24:1–12. Why do you search for the living among the dead?

Easter Sunday

All cycles. John 20:1–9. He is risen!

Preparation for the Drama

(See resource intro–A, "Leader's Tasks.")

Roles

Catechist, who coordinates the drama
Lector, who leads the opening prayer and proclaims the sacred Scriptures
Gospel players, who enflesh the roles in the scriptural drama

- Guard 1
- Guard 2
- Mary of Magdala
- Salome
- Mary the Wife of Clopas
- Joanna the Wife of Chuza
- Mary the Mother of James and John (nonspeaking role)
- Angel of the Resurrection
- Jesus
- Andrew
- James the Son of Zebedee
- Mark
- Peter
- John
- Matthew

Costume Trunk Items

A lectionary or Bible, Roman guard uniforms and spears, robes, headdresses, veils, cloaks, a jar of oil, a rolled-up face cloth, a shroud, and a white robe and wings (for the angel; a white lace cloth can be held up as the wings)

Presentation of the Drama
(See resource intro–A, "Leader's Tasks.")

Script for the Background Reading

Catechist. When Jesus died on the tree of Calvary, the Sabbath was drawing near. His followers had to bury him immediately for three reasons. First, they could not work on the Sabbath because it honors the gift of rest and commemorates the rest of God after the work of Creation. Second, according to Jewish Law, even a criminal's body had to be buried on the day of death. And third, according to Roman law, if the family of a crucified criminal did not claim the body for burial, dogs would be allowed to eat the remains.

Jesus was from Galilee. None of his loved ones had a tomb in Jerusalem. This added to their profound grief. Joseph of Arimathea, a member of the Sanhedrin and a secret follower of Christ's, convinced Pilate to give him the body of Jesus, and provided a tomb that he had carved for himself out of a cave in a rock.

Nicodemus and Joseph carried the lifeless body of Jesus to the cemetery. There they quickly and without ceremony wrapped it in a linen shroud and laid it on a shelf in the rock tomb. Because the sun was setting, by Law they did not have time to properly prepare the body. So the tomb was closed with a huge stone set at the mouth of the cave.

As the sun set into a desert of darkness, so did the hopes of Jesus' followers. Their grief was so profound that the entire creation mourned.

Script for the Gospel Reading

[The lector leads everyone in prayer while holding up a lectionary or Bible for all to see.]

Lector. Lord, we ask you to fill us with the power and courage of the Holy Spirit. Make us unafraid to proclaim with Mary of Magdala, "He is risen!"

[The lector proclaims the appropriate Gospel reading for the current cycle from the lectionary or Bible. Upon finishing, the lector leads the group in response to the Gospel, again holding up the lectionary or Bible for all to see.]

Lector. Alleluia!

Group. Alleluia!

Script for the Gospel Drama

[The catechist announces to the group the title of the Gospel scene to be dramatized.]

Catechist. "He Is Risen"

[The catechist describes the Gospel scene to the group.]

Catechist. Mary of Magdala, Salome, Mary the wife of Clopas, Joanna the wife of Chuza, and Mary the mother of James and John stood at the foot of the cross. They were at the tomb when Jesus was laid in it. And on this first Easter morning, they will be the first to share in the glory of the Resurrection.

As the Sabbath draws to a close, those women go to the tomb intending to anoint the body of their beloved Lord, to cleanse the horror of the Crucifixion from his body, to prepare Jesus for eternal rest. Here at the tomb of the Christ is the darkest moment in all of creation, yet the power and love of God re-create all things new. Nothing can destroy what God has willed. The day of the Lord will come to be. In the first light of dawn, all that is . . . is made new. In the first moments that they realize the tomb is empty, as grief turns to resurrected joy, these first disciples of the Christ reflect the mission of all of us who follow him. The women at the tomb are encouraged by the angel of the Lord to *believe,* to *proclaim* what they have experienced, and to *rejoice.*

At the darkest moments of our lives, the love of God is still the greater reality. Emmanuel is with us, ready to offer new life, new hope, and Easter joy.

Guard 1. This darkness tonight is so strange.

Guard 2. The cold stillness gives me the creeps. Stop talking about it. It will be dawn soon.

Guard 1. Talk about strange! Why are the authorities so worried about this poor guy, even in his tomb? Why do we have to guard his body?

Guard 2. I heard that they are afraid his followers will come and steal his body and claim he is alive, and start a cult. Whatever did he do to be so hated and feared by the government?

Guard 1. It doesn't take much to be accused of treason.

Guard 2. You better watch your tongue or you'll be next. Is it possible that it's getting even darker around here?

Guard 1. I don't want to think about it . . . So what are you going to do when you're off duty?

Guard 2. Go into town, get some wine and a girl.

[Mary of Magdala, Salome, and Mary the wife of Clopas approach the tomb. Joanna the wife of Chuza and Mary the mother of James and John stay back in the shadows.]

Guard 1. Here come a couple of women right now.

Guard 2. I count three of them. But look in the shadows . . . there's more.

Guard 1. They don't look like they're in the mood for a party. Yo! Ladies! What is happening?

Guard 2. Women! You're not permitted here! No one is permitted here until sunrise. Pilate's order. Go home for a few hours.

Mary of Magdala. Please, sir. I've caused you no harm. I've been here all night, watching in grief from the shadows. Let us stay with our Lord.

Salome. Let us be near to Jesus. He is our Lord.

Mary of Magdala. *[Holding out a jar of oil]* I've brought spiced oil to anoint Jesus, to prepare his body for eternal rest.

Mary the Wife of Clopas. Sabbath is over. It is our custom.

Joanna the Wife of Chuza. *[Coming out of the shadows with Mary the Mother of James and John]* We need to purify the body of our Rabbi.

Salome. Please be merciful, sire. Our hearts have failed us; grief overcomes us.

Mary the Wife of Clopas. Let us come to the tomb.

Guard 1. Well, we have our orders, ma'am.

Guard 2. And we have been paid well.

Mary of Magdala. Where is the body of my Lord?

Guard 1. He's right in this tomb, but don't think we're going to let you near him.

Guard 2. *[Laughing]* That's right; we were warned that some of his disciples might want to steal the body away.

[A great rumbling is heard, and the earth quakes.]

Guard 1. What is that? Mercy from the gods, it's an earthquake!

Guard 2. We will be killed. Hide under this ledge.

Guard 1. Look at the tomb. The stone has been rolled back. What is happening here?

Mary of Magdala. Who could have moved that heavy stone? *[Mary looks into the tomb, which is empty except for a rolled-up face cloth and a shroud.]* Where is my Lord? Jesus is gone! Where have they taken his body?

[The angel of the Resurrection appears in front of the tomb.]

Guard 2. Who is that man? His face is like lightning!

Guard 1. Dressed white as snow. I think we're dead men. Let's get out of here.

Guard 2. Run as fast as you can! My legs shake. I don't think I can move.

Angel of the Resurrection. Woman, why are you weeping? Do not be afraid. I know that you are looking for Jesus, who was crucified.

Mary of Magdala. They've taken my Lord away . . . I don't know where he is . . . I don't know where they've taken his body.

Angel. He is not here. Come, see the place where he lay.

Mary of Magdala. I've brought oil to anoint him. Where have they taken my Lord?

Angel. He is not here. Woman, do you remember what he said to you, while he was still in Galilee: that the Son of man had to be betrayed into the hands of sinful men and that he had to be crucified, and that on the third day he would rise again?

Mary of Magdala. I remember and I am a witness that this has happened. I love him so. Please! Where have you taken my Lord?!

Angel. Woman, why do you search for the living among the dead?

[Jesus approaches the tomb.]

Mary of Magdala. I'm so confused by all this. *[Spotting Jesus but not recognizing him]* Sire, Gardener! Do you know where they have taken my Lord?

Jesus. Mary!

Angel. This Jesus is living! He is risen . . . as he said!

Mary of Magdala. Rabboni! What is this?! Lord, is this you?

Jesus. Do not hold on to me, because I have not yet ascended to the Father. But go to my brothers, Mary, and tell them I am ascending to my Father and your Father, to my God and your God.

Mary of Magdala. Rabboni! Jesus!

Angel. Shout for joy, Daughter of Zion. Israel, shout aloud! Rejoice! Sing with all your heart! Daughters of Jerusalem—the Lord has repealed your sentence!

Mary of Magdala. Rabboni! HE IS RISEN! Alleluia! I have seen the Lord! Christ is risen! Jesus lives!

Catechist. The readings in this week's liturgy celebrate both the Resurrection of Jesus and the healing of the community from its lack of faith. Above the head of Jesus, as he hung on the cross of execution, the Roman guard posted these words: "Jesus the Christ, King of the Jews." The Romans had sentenced Jesus to death for trying to establish a new kingdom with a new king. Jesus' followers are sure the authorities suspect that they were part of his treasonous movement.

   With Jesus dead, most of his Apostles have locked themselves in the house where they ate the Last Supper. They know the patterns of Roman control: all the followers of Jesus will likely be put to death in the weeks following the Crucifixion of the Christ. As they cower in the upper room, hiding from the Roman guards and trembling in fear of their own approaching deaths, Mary of Magdala arrives to proclaim the Resurrection.

[Mary enters, followed by Peter and John, who are both out of breath.]

Mary of Magdala. Brothers, I have seen him! I have seen the Lord! He is risen, as he said . . . Do you hear me? I have seen Jesus. He lives! He told me to tell you—he is risen. Alleluia.

Andrew. The idle talk of women! Who could believe her?

Mary of Magdala. Andrew! I have seen him! I have seen the Lord!

Andrew. Listen to the woman babble. Obviously she is fevered and insane.

James the Son of Zebedee. Listen, we're in enough trouble as it is. We don't need you running off at the mouth about seeing ghosts.

Mark. Not only will the Romans think we're traitors, they'll think we're a bunch of nuts. Who could believe you, Mary?

Mary of Magdala. Brothers, he has sent me to tell you. I have seen the Lord! And not only me, but your mother, James.

James. My mother? My mother saw him?

Mary of Magdala. And Joanna the wife of Herod's steward, and Salome, and Mary the wife of Clopas as well. We all saw the empty tomb. We saw and heard the angel. The angel said he lives, as the Roman guards trembled in fear. And we saw and heard the risen Jesus, who has sent me to tell you *he is risen!* Alleluia!

Peter. Why wouldn't it be true? Didn't he tell us that on the third day he would rise? I believe her. I myself, with John, ran to the tomb when we heard the news. We saw that the stone had been moved back and the tomb was empty.

John. The shroud that Joseph of Arimathea and Nicodemus had wrapped him in was lying there.

Peter. The face cloth was rolled up and placed to the side.

Matthew. Did you see Jesus, Peter?

Peter. No.

Matthew. John, did you see him?

John. No.

Peter. No, but we believe. We believe the testimony of those women, whom he loved.

James. Women by law cannot be official witnesses or offer testimony anywhere in the Roman Empire. Why would Jesus choose them to witness his Resurrection?

Peter. Why would he choose me? I denied him three times—like the coward that I am. Why would he choose any of us? Look at us hiding here like terrified cowards! Why shouldn't we believe Mary? Did we have any faith at all? He said he would return. He taught us the truth of eternal life and proclaimed the resurrection of the dead. Why should we not believe him?

Mary of Magdala. Why do you hide like wanted criminals, in this upper room, terrified of the Romans? Have courage, brothers; I have seen the Lord! Brothers, believe in him and see the salvation of God. My Jesus lives. Christ is alive—he conquered the darkness. Shout the Good News to the ends of the earth: Jesus lives!

Catechist. Later that day, Jesus appears in the upper room—even though the doors are all bolted—and stands before his disciples. He shows them the scars in his hands and his side, and they rejoice at the sight of him. What does Jesus say to these friends who abandoned him in his darkest hour? He does not say: "Where were you when I needed you? What kind of friends are you?" He looks at them with much love and says "Peace!"

Jesus. Peace be with you! As the Father has sent me, I also send you. Receive the Holy Spirit.

Catechist. All over the Christian world, the universal community of Christ gathers to celebrate the Resurrection of the Lord at Easter. How fitting that the memorial of Passover, in which the angel of death passed over the houses of the Israelites, becomes the greatest Christian feast, honoring Christ's victory over death for all time. The darkness of oppression and the slavery of sin are shattered against the light of Christ. The grace of salvation that is offered through the heart of Christ Jesus delivers the children of the earth from everything and anything that steals the joy that God intends for them. In every Eucharist, at every liturgy of the Mass until the end of time, we pray, "Dying you destroyed our death, / rising you restored our life."

On that first Easter morning, the resurrected Christ stood among his followers. He appeared in glory, yet every scar of the Passion was visible. Jesus didn't hide the evidence of Calvary. But he transformed the wounds into badges of honor. We are invited to do the same. As he called those original disciples, he calls us to believe, to proclaim, and to rejoice in the gift of salvation. He empowers us to heal the wounds of life and fill every grief with the salve of salvation. This becomes the great mission of the church. You and I, as followers of the Christ, are commissioned by our baptism to proclaim this Good News to the end of time. Nothing is more powerful than love. The love of Jesus, crucified and resurrected, sets us free.

Jesus. All power is given to me in heaven and on earth. Go. Teach this Good News to the whole creation—to every ethnic group, every nation—and offer all of humanity the salvation of God. Baptize all people in the name of the Father, and of the Son, and of the Holy Spirit. Teach my law of love. Remember always that I am with you until the end of the world. Peace be with you. *I go before you . . . always . . . until the end of time.*

Follow-up After the Drama
(See resource intro–A, "Leader's Tasks.")

Reflection Questions

- The authorities had exercised all their power to eliminate Jesus, to erase him from history. They had used treachery, an illegal sentence, a slanderous charge, and ultimately bribery to silence the truth. There is an ancient Roman proverb, "Great is the truth and it will prevail." How does the Resurrection of Jesus point to that proverb?
- Jesus had promised that he would rise victoriously on the third day after his death, but amid his Passion and death, the faith of his followers was tested to the limit. What does this tell you about the dark moments in life when you feel alone and discouraged and all hope seems lost?

- The Apostle Thomas was not present in the upper room the first time Jesus appeared after his death. Thomas refused to believe in Christ's Resurrection until later when he was able to personally touch the wounds in Jesus' hands and side. Jesus said then: "Thomas, you have believed because you have seen. Blessed are those who have not seen, and yet believe." If you are among those who believe in Christ without having seen him with your own eyes, Christ calls you blessed. What does that mean to you?

- Life and death run through all of earthly reality, and both are necessary for growth and transformation. Out of Christ's death came new life. Through baptism, we share in this life, which will continue past death into eternity. Jesus promised: "Unless a grain of wheat falls to the ground and dies, it remains just a single grain; but if it dies, it brings forth much fruit. People who love their life will lose it, but people who hate their life in this world will keep it forever." In the light of the Resurrection story, what does that paradox mean to you?

- The following beautiful prayer from Saint Francis captures the spirit of Easter joy. Reflect on the words of this prayer. Then share some ideas of how we can put them into action today.

> Lord, make me an instrument of your peace.
>> Where there is hatred, let me sow love,
>> Where there is injury, pardon;
>> Where there is doubt, faith;
>> Where there is despair, hope;
>> Where there is darkness, light;
>> And where there is sadness, joy.
>
> O, Divine Master, grant that I may not so much
>> seek to be consoled as to console,
>> to be understood as to understand,
>> to be loved, as to love.
>
> For it is in giving that we receive,
>> it is in pardoning that we are pardoned,
>> and it is in dying that we are born to eternal life.

Improv
(See resource intro–A, "Leader's Tasks.")

Closure
(See resource intro–A, "Leader's Tasks.")

Easter Sunday Icon

The Resurrection of Jesus Christ from the dead is an awesome mystery to consider. Following the Way of Jesus brings us also to transformation and new life. All cycles: John 20:1–9

Bibliography

Books

Brown, Raymond E., Joseph A. Fitzmyer, and Roland E. Murphy, editors. *The New Jerome Biblical Commentary*. Englewood Cliffs, NJ: Prentice-Hall, 1990.

Flannery, Austin, editor. *Vatican Council II: The Conciliar and Post Conciliar Documents*. New revised edition. Grand Rapids, MI: William B. Eerdmans Publishing Company, 1992.

Komonchak, Joseph A., Mary Collins, and Dermot A. Lane. *The New Dictionary of Theology*. Collegeville, MN: Liturgical Press, Michael Glazier Books, 1991.

Malina, Bruce J., and Richard L. Rohrbaugh. *Social-Science Commentary on the Gospel of John*. Minneapolis: Augsburg Fortress Publishers, 1998.

———. *Social-Science Commentary on the Synoptic Gospels*. Minneapolis: Augsburg Fortress, 1992.

McKenzie, John L. *The Dictionary of the Bible*. New York: Macmillan Publishing, 1965.

Metzger, Bruce M., and Michael D. Coogan, editors. *The Oxford Companion to the Bible*. New York: Oxford University Press, 1993.

O'Connell-Roussell, Sheila. *The Word Is Made Flesh: The Sacred Art of Theatre*. Bend, OR: Amnchara Cruces, 1999.

O'Connell-Roussell, Sheila, and Terri Vorndran Nichols. *Lectionary-Based Gospel Dramas for Advent, Christmas, and Epiphany*. Winona, MN: Saint Mary's Press, 1997.

Scripts

O'Connell-Roussell, Sheila, and Terri Vorndran Nichols. *Back to Eden*. Bend, OR: Roger Nichols Music, 1992.

———. *Herstory: The Mother's Tale*. Bend, OR: Roger Nichols Music, 1992.

Sound Recordings

O'Connell-Roussell, Sheila. *Back to Eden*. Bend, OR: Spirit Records, Roger Nichols Music, 1992. Compact disk and audiotape.

O'Connell-Roussell, Sheila, and Elinore O'Connell. *Herstory: The Mother's Tale*. Bend, OR: Spirit Records, Roger Nichols Music, 1992. Compact disk and audiotape.

Videotape

Nichols, Terri Vorndran, Roger Nichols, and Sheila O'Connell-Roussell. *Herstory: The Mother's Tale.* Bend, OR: Roger Nichols Studios, 1993.

Software

Barclay's Commentary, 1997. Liguori Publications, Liguori, Mo.

The Bible Library for Catholics, 1996. Liguori Publications, Liguori, Mo. All Scripture passages are adapted from the New Revised Standard Version of the Bible.

Preach and Teach: Anecdotes, Stories, and Quotes, 1994. Liguori Publications, Liguori, Mo.

Strongs Exhaustive Concordance of the Bible, 1996. Liguori Publications, Liguori, Mo.

Gospel Readings for the Lent and Easter Triduum Dramas

First Sunday of Lent

Cycle A. Matthew 4:1–11. Tempted in the desert: preparation for the mission.
Cycle B. Mark 1:12–15. Put to the test: temptation in the desert.
Cycle C. Luke 4:1–13. Led by the Spirit: forty days and forty nights.

Second Sunday of Lent

Cycle A. Matthew 17:1–9. Transformed before their eyes.
Cycle B. Mark 9:2–10. The Transfiguration: Jesus, the Son of man.
Cycle C. Luke 9:28–36. Moses and Elijah proclaim the glory of God.

Third Sunday of Lent

Cycle A. John 4:5–42. The Samaritan woman at the well: Living Water.
Cycle B. John 2:13–25. My Father's house: warning the sellers in the Temple.

Fourth Sunday of Lent

Cycle A. John, chapter 9. Healing of the blind: the Light of the World.
Cycle B. John 3:14–21. Believing offers eternal life.

Fifth Sunday of Lent

Cycle A. John 11:1–45. The resurrection of Lazarus.
Cycle B. John 12:20–33. We want to see Jesus.

Passion Sunday, or Palm Sunday

Cycle A. Matthew 21:1–11. Daughter of Zion, your king comes to you.
Cycle B. Mark 11:1–10. Hosanna! Blessed is he who comes in the name of the Lord.
Cycle C. Luke 19:28–40. The very stones would cry out!

Holy Thursday

All cycles. John 13:1–5. Jesus washes the feet of the disciples.

Good Friday

Passion Sunday, or Palm Sunday

Cycle A. Matthew 26:14–27,66. The Passion of Jesus Christ.
Cycle B. Mark 14:1–47. The Passion of Jesus Christ.
Cycle C. Luke 22:14–56. The Passion of Jesus Christ.

Good Friday

All cycles. John, chapters 18–19. Arrest, judgment, death, and burial.

Holy Saturday and Easter Sunday

Holy Saturday

Cycle A. Matthew 28:1–10. Go tell the brothers. He is risen!
Cycle B. Mark 16:1–8. Who rolled back the stone?
Cycle C. Luke 24:1–12. Why do you search for the living among the dead?

Easter Sunday

All cycles. John 20:1–9. He is risen!